THE NATIONAL LEAGUE

THE
NATIONAL
LEAGUE
A HISTORY

JOEL ZOSS AND JOHN S. BOWMAN

SMITHMARK

This edition published in 1995
by SMITHMARK Publishers Inc.,
16 East 32nd Street
New York, New York 10016.

SMITHMARK books are available for bulk purchase for sales promotion
and premium use. For details write or telephone the Manager of Special
Sales, SMITHMARK Publishers Inc., 16 East 32nd Street, New York, NY
10016. (212) 532-6600.

Produced by Brompton Books Corp.
15 Sherwood Place,
Greenwich, CT 06830

ISBN 0-8317-6757-X

Printed in Spain

10 9 8 7 6 5 4 3 2 1

Revised and updated 1995

CONTENTS

CHAPTER ONE

In the Beginning

The wit of man cannot devise a plan or frame a form of government that will control the game of baseball for over five years.

William Ambrose Hulbert, founder of the National League

The National League of Professional Base Ball Clubs was founded on 2 February 1876, almost exactly one hundred years after the founding of the United States. The game had long since become the fledgling democracy's national pastime and obsession, but in 1876 few even of its most ardent supporters would have guessed that by the time another hundred years had passed baseball would be a billion-dollar-a-year business with over 50 million paying spectators annually and star players signing multi-year contracts for upwards of $20 million.

The development of baseball is the story of 19th-century America in microcosm. While the country was changing from a rural society into a nation of large cities, baseball developed from the children's game of rounders to a highly skilled game of professionals performing for the entertainment of paying spectators. In between, it was played by all kinds and classes of people. Dr. Oliver Wendell Holmes writes of playing baseball on a diamond-shaped field at Harvard in 1829. By the 1840s, the basic pattern of the game was being shaped in amateur clubs founded by young professionals in Eastern cities.

The Knickerbocker Base Ball Club of New York City, one of the first amateur clubs to have a real organization, appointed a committee to standardize the rules of the game for intra- and intermural competition. Their code, adopted on 23 September 1845, stands as something of a landmark in baseball history. Significantly, the Knickerbocker rules decreed that a player could no longer be put out by being hit with a thrown ball. In a game played between the Knickerbockers and the New York Nine in New Jersey in 1846, the Knicks were badly trounced, and player J W Davis was fined six cents for swearing at the umpire. Games played by these early amateur clubs were highly social occasions; often the losing team paid for the banquet that followed.

The rules codified by the Knickerbockers were adopted by many other clubs, and the 'New York Game' became the basis for intercity competition. During the 1850s something like a national mania grew up around these amateur clubs. Seasoned observers of the contemporary scene were amazed at baseball's success, and on 10 March 1858 representatives from 25 of the more than 100 clubs in the North formed the first league, the National Association of Base Ball Players. Brooklyn and Manhattan teams played an All-Star game on 20 July 1858, charging 50 cents admission to cover the costs of preparing the grounds. This was the first time admission was charged in the history of the game. Baseball was still amateur, but was on its way to becoming a commercialized amusement.

The Civil War dampened baseball enthusiasm for a while, and many of the clubs from New York to Chicago went under. But the war also did much to spread the gospel of baseball. On Christmas Day 1862, a throng of 40,000 Union soldiers – probably the largest crowd for any sporting event in the 19th century – watched a game between two Union All-Star teams. After the war, baseball mania returned to top prewar excesses. Professional and commercial interests began to realize that profits could be wrung from baseball promotion. By the late 1860s, the gentlemanly amateur code which governed the sport had given way to the ethic of winning, and gentlemen and children were no longer the only players. As Theodore Roosevelt later remarked, 'When money comes in at the gate, sport flies out the window.' Many businesses hired young men to work in their industries with a

Page 1: Cardinal shortstop Ozzie Smith.
Pages 2-3: Three-time Cy Young Award winner Greg Maddux of the Atlanta Braves.
Pages 4-5: Cardinals' Gas House Gang member Pepper Martin takes a head-first slide.
Below: Some New York Knickerbockers, circa 1847.

view toward using their baseball talents in the teams they sponsored. When such teams began traveling, taking on all comers, amateurism became a sham.

In 1869, Harry Wright, a professional cricket player and English-born son of a cricket professional, organized the first all-salaried professional team, the Cincinnati Reds (Red Stockings). Their astounding success against amateurs transformed baseball in America. Professional interests met in New York to establish the first professional league, the National Association of Professional Base-Ball Players, in 1871. This league was not always able to make players live up to their contracts and clubs to their schedules, but during its five years of existence it did much to broaden the game's appeal.

By the mid-1870s, baseball was booming, but the National Association clubs were so riddled with heavy gambling, game-throwing, drunkenness, player desertion, contract-jumping and plain rowdiness on both sides of the dugout that public confidence in the integrity and character of the game was reaching a dangerous point. William Ambrose Hulbert, a Chicago businessman and president of the Chicago National Association club, feared for professional baseball's future as much as he was excited by its potential, and decided to do something about it.

Joining forces with Boston superstar pitcher Al Spalding, whom he enticed to his Chicago Club for the 1876 season along with the rest of Boston's famous 'Big Four' infield, Hulbert concluded that the reforms necessary for baseball to survive and thrive could not be effected within the existing structure of the rickety National Association, and decided to form a new league to be called the 'National League of Professional Base Ball Clubs.' At a secret meeting in Louisville in January 1876, Hulbert sold his scheme to representatives of the St Louis, Cincinnati and Louisville baseball clubs. Moving east, on 2 February 1876 he met with representatives of Boston, Hartford, Philadelphia and New York at the Grand Central Hotel in New York. Hulbert reportedly locked the hotel room door while he read the proposed constitution and player contract he and Spalding had prepared. The Easterners, equally worried about the effects of gam-

bling and other evils, unanimously agreed to the formation of a new league. Morgan P Bulkeley of Hartford was chosen president of a five-man committee which would control the new organization, and the National League was born.

Hulbert and Spalding's constitution has provided the basis of the National League – as well as the blueprint for professional sport in this country – for more than a century. The National League's objectives were to encourage, foster and elevate the game of baseball; to enact and enforce proper rules for the exhibition and conduct of the game and to make baseball-playing respectable and honorable. The constitution forbade gambling and the sale of alcohol on the grounds, obligated each team to play a complete schedule, and required each franchise to represent a city of at least 75,000. Above all, Hulbert wanted a league that would be profitable, run in a disciplined, businesslike manner. To this end the control of the game was to be placed firmly in the hands of the owners, rather than the players. Players were bound to one club by an ingenious reserve clause (finally approved in 1879) which guaranteed a club a player's services for as long as it wished, and were no longer to have any voice in the operation of the league. Gone were the days when contracts were broken almost at will, and players convicted of throwing games experienced virtually no difficulty in finding employment with other clubs.

The first game of the new league was played in Philadelphia on 22 April 1876, with Boston defeating Philadelphia, 6-5. Each of the eight charter teams was scheduled to meet every other team ten times between 15 March and 15 November (five games at home and five away), league games taking place three times a week. Admission was set at 50 cents, reduced to ten cents after the third inning. Each club had to provide a sufficient number of police to preserve order. Dues were set at $100 annually, ten times what they had been in the National Association. The team winning the most games would receive a pennant costing not less than $100.

The first no-hitter in National League history was recorded on 15 July 1876 by George Washington

Bradley of St Louis, who blanked Hartford, 2-0. A strong Chicago club took the pennant, followed in order of wins by Hartford, St Louis, Boston, Louisville, New York, Philadelphia and Cincinnati.

Paid attendance was not high enough to ensure financial success that first season, but at least gambling and liquor sales were down. The league's first test occurred when New York and Philadelphia, fearing financial loss, declared themselves more important to the league than the league was to them, and refused to make their final western trip. Much to their astonishment, Hulbert, who had replaced Bulkeley as president in December, proved the league meant business and as his first official action expelled the two clubs from the league.

The 1877 season began with six clubs. The 'fair-foul' rule was eliminated – a ball hit foul but which rolled fair between home and first or third was now forever foul – and the infant league met its second great test when it became clear late in the season that four players from the strong Louisville team were throwing games for big-time New York gamblers. The players confessed, and all were banished forever from organized ball.

Boston and Chicago were the only charter clubs remaining in the league at the start of the 1878 season, but Cincinnati soon made up past dues and bought its way back in, and clubs from Providence, Indianapolis and Milwaukee rounded out the circuit. Because of its swift and firm action against the Louisville gamblers,

the league enjoyed a new respect from the public and the press alike. That year Boston offered season tickets, turnstiles were introduced and the ambiguity surrounding Sunday games was eliminated when the league adopted a rule to expel clubs that violated the Sabbath or failed to expel players who did. Crowds of 6000 fans flocked to see games in Boston and Providence.

The first 25 years tested the courage of the National League's pioneers time and time again. There was a constant shifting of franchises during this period, and many fortunes were made and lost. While Chicago and Boston maintained their uninterrupted presence on the circuit, up until 1900, when the league settled into the same eight franchises it would maintain for the next 53 years, teams from 23 cities came and went, including Providence, Milwaukee, Indianapolis, Buffalo, Cleveland, Troy, Syracuse, Worcester, Detroit, Kansas City, Washington, Baltimore, Brooklyn, Pittsburgh and New York.

The new league also soon found itself involved in costly wars with other organizations. In 1882, the American Association of Base Ball Clubs, also known as the 'Beer-Ball League,' featuring Sunday games, a 25-cent admission, and sale of alcoholic beverages on the grounds, was formed to compete with the National League. Under the farsighted presidency of the National League's President A G Mills, the American Association eventually signed an agreement with the National League, and the two leagues held post-

Below: The Providence team poses for a portrait before an 1879 game.

season World Series which contributed greatly to baseball's popularity.

Baseball didn't really settle into the game it is today until the turn of the century. Before 1887, batters could request a high or a low pitch. After several changes, the distance from pitcher to batter was finally lengthened to the present 60-feet-six-inches in 1893. Pitchers were not permitted to throw overhand until 1883, a date some claim marks the birth of modern baseball, and a staff of umpires with fixed salaries was appointed for the first time in the same year. The nine balls necessary for a batter to walk were reduced to five in 1887, and finally four in 1889. Strikeouts, originally set at five, were reduced to three in 1888, but foul tips did not count as strikes until 1895, and foul balls didn't count as strikes until 1901. In 1903 a foul tip caught after two strikes became an out. Before 1891, substitutions were permitted only in the case of injury or with the other team's permission. Walks were counted as hits the first season, and stolen base statistics credited runners for each base advanced on another player's hit until 1898. The ball itself, of course, was much less lively than it would later become. From 1894 through 1897, first and second place clubs battled for a gaudy trophy known as the Temple Cup.

By far the most important ingredient in baseball's success was the new public hero, the baseball star, whose magnetic presence could be counted upon to lure city dwellers to the ball parks. Primarily a product of keen competition between National League clubs, the baseball hero was also very much the creation of baseball sportswriters. It was this new breed of specialists in American journalism who in the 1880s helped turn major-league baseball into a million-dollar industry. Henry Chadwick long dominated the trade, but younger writers created the breezy, cliché-ridden copy which still characterizes this unique form of American literature.

Chicago and Boston thoroughly dominated the first

Michael Joseph 'King' Kelly, who broke in with Cincinnati in 1878, then went to Chicago to play from 1880 to 1889. After moving to Boston for three years, he was lured to the Players' League Boston club, where he was player-manager for two years. In 1892 he returned to the Boston National League club and then switched to New York in 1893 – his final year. He was elected to the Hall of Fame in 1945.

11 years of National League life. The Chicago White Stockings took six pennants by 1886, five under the leadership of Adrian Anson, one of the greatest players in baseball history and perhaps the outstanding player in the National League in its first quarter century. Signing with Chicago in 1876, the six-foot-two, two-hundred pound 'Cap' or 'Pop' Anson was a fearsome hitter who batted over .300 for 20 of his 22 seasons with the club, and was as popular as any player until Babe Ruth. Anson lured thousands to games with his genius for showmanship, and was an early adept at vilifying the umpire, a form of ritualized hostility which, to the delight of promoters and writers, flowered in the 1880s, turning umpires into evil black-suited villains who attracted crowds to the park as much as the new baseball heroes.

Shortly after the end of his career with Chicago in 1898, Anson entered vaudeville, but at his death in 1922 he was still known as the 'Grand Old Man of Baseball.' His funeral was one of the largest ever accorded an athlete in this country, and he was elected to the Hall of Fame in 1939.

After he was appointed Chicago's playing manager in 1879, Anson's influence on how the game was played became incalculable. The White Stockings won five pennants in his first seven years of management, including three in a row, 1880-1882. Fans of this era thrilled to the deeds of Chicago's pitching ace Larry Corcoran, of third baseman Ed Williamson, who hit an amazing 27 home runs in 1884, of pitcher John Clarkson, catcher Silver Flint, Abner Dalrymple, George Gore, Fred Goldsmith and many others. Cap himself hit five home runs in two consecutive games in 1884, a record that has since been tied but never surpassed. In the 13-year period 1880-1892, Anson's White Stockings never finished lower than fourth place.

Anson was a famous disciplinarian. He instituted a $100 fine for beer drinking on his club and conducted nightly bed checks. Among his many managerial innovations, Anson, who took the White Stockings to Hot Springs, Arkansas, in 1885, is generally credited as the first to take a team south for spring training. At a time when baseball strategy was in its infancy, he pioneered the 'scientific' game, drilling his teams in offensive and defensive signals, and experimenting with pitching rotation, alternating fast-baller Larry Corcoran and slow-baller Fred Goldsmith with great effectiveness. He taught his outfielders to back up infielders, sometimes platooned his players, and was among the first, with Mike 'Slide, Kelly, Slide' Kelly, to use the hit-and-run.

Among his heavy hitters and speedy base runners was Fred Pfeffer, who once ran the bases in less than 16 seconds. Billy Sunday, the future evangelist, best at stealing bases in an outstanding 1886 season, and 'King' Kelly captivated crowds with the same flamboyance as their manager. Kelly once won a close game from Boston by cutting from second to home, correctly calculating that the lone umpire used in those days would miss his shortcut.

Not all of Anson's influence on the game was good. His racism left an ugly mark for years to come. In the 1880s, quite a few blacks – at least twenty – played ball with white clubs, despite an 1867 National Association resolution which barred blacks and clubs they played for from membership. The National Association of Professional Base Ball Players, which succeeded the original National Association in 1871, never had a written rule, but an ironclad 'gentlemen's agreement' barred blacks and black clubs. The force

of this unwritten law carried over into the National League. Nevertheless, the color line did not have universal support in the majors. Moses Fleetwood Walker and his brother William Welday Walker, for instance, both played with Toledo in the American Association, which was a major league at the time. Fleetwood Walker later played for a Newark team which included George Stovey, whom some consider the greatest black pitcher of all time.

In 1883, when the White Stockings played an exhibition game against Toledo, Anson saw Fleetwood Walker on the diamond and yelled with characteristic tact, 'Get that nigger off the field!' Anson swallowed his refusal not to play when he was informed that his team would forfeit the gate, but five years later he once again refused to play against a Newark club which included George Stovey. Stovey walked off and refused to play the White Stockings.

In 1887, at a time when it looked like blacks would slowly but surely enter white organized baseball's structure, John Montgomery Ward decided to bring Stovey up to pitch for the Giants, an act that would have broken the color barrier long before Jackie Robinson was born. Anson got wind of his plan, and mustered industry pressure to force Ward to change

his mind, using all his tremendous popularity and prestige in baseball circles. Bellowing 'There's a law against that,' Anson succeeded in setting a precedent, and can claim credit for almost singlehandedly excluding the black man from major-league baseball until 1947.

Under baseball pioneer Harry Wright, Boston took the pennant in 1877 and again in 1878. Boston's winning lineup in those years included such outstanding players as Jim O'Rourke, pitcher Tom Bond – who won 40 games in 1877 and in 1878 – George Wright, Jim Morrill and Jim White, top batter of 1877. Boston came back to end Chicago's three-year pennant streak by taking the flag again in 1883.

Providence, which had last taken a pennant in 1879, captured the flag again in 1884, although Anson's White Stockings returned to lead the league in 1885 and 1886. Providence's 1884 win was carried by the incredible pitching of Charles 'Old Hoss' Radbourne, who won 60 of the 75 games he pitched that year, losing 12, for a 1.38 ERA. That season Radbourne had been suspended early on by manager F C Bancroft. Both were difficult men. When Radbourne's services were required, he announced he would pitch every game and Providence would win the flag, but only if

Above: John Montgomery 'Monte' Ward when he was the captain of the New York club. Elected to the Hall of Fame in 1964, he also played for Providence and Brooklyn.
Above left: William Henry 'Harry' Wright of the Boston club, elected to the Hall of Fame in 1953. Oddly enough, he was born in Sheffield, England.
Inset: Charles Gardner 'Old Hoss' Radbourn when he played for the Boston Beaneaters (1886-1889). He also played for Providence, Buffalo, Cincinnati and the Boston Players' League team, and was elected to the Hall of Fame in 1939.

Above: A team portrait of the 1882 Detroit Wolverines.
Far right: Amos Wilson Rusie – 'The Hoosier Thunderbolt' – a pitcher who started with Indianapolis in 1889, then went to New York from 1890 to 1898, finishing his career with Cincinnati in 1901. His lifetime record of 243-160, his earned run average of 3.07 and his 1957 strikeouts earned him a place in the Hall of Fame in 1977.

the directors lifted his suspension and agreed to release him at the end of the season. They did.

Radbourne proceeded to pitch in all but two of his team's last 37 games. From 23 July to 7 August he pitched in nine consecutive games, winning seven and tying one. He took a day off to play right field, then pitched and won six consecutive games. He took off another day to play shortstop, and beginning on 21 August pitched in the next 20 games, winning ten before losing to Buffalo on 9 September, the defeat ending a 16-game winning streak for Radbourne and a 20-game winning streak for his team. Providence finished ten games ahead of second-place Boston, and 'Lord' Radbourne, whose Hall of Fame plaque calls him the 'greatest of the 19th century pitchers,' easily beat the New York Metropolitans in the first official World Series.

The Detroit Wolverines, spearheaded by catcher Charles Bennett and Captain Ned Hanlon, took the pennant in 1887, terrorizing the league with their hitting. Detroit's team batting average for 1887 was .343. The lineup featured Johnny Rowe, Charley Getzein and Charley Ganzel – the 'pretzel battery' – and Dan Brouthers, one of the greatest batters of all times. Brouthers batted over .300 fourteen times, playing professional ball until until he was 48. In the 1887 season both Brouthers and teammate Sam Thompson hit over .400 (in those days a base on balls was credited as a hit), and Brouthers managed at least one base or its equivalent in 107 out of his 122 games.

The New York Giants, who returned to the league with Philadelphia in 1883, took flags in 1888 and 1889 under stovepipe-hatted Jim Mutrie. His teams featured pitcher Jim Keefe, who won 19 in a row, outstanding catcher Buck Ewing, Roger Connor and hurler Micky Welch. Welch, who once fanned the first nine men he faced in a game, credited his pitching prowess to beer: 'Pure elixir of malt and hops/Beats all the drugs and all the drops.'

1889 saw the closest race yet in the National League's 14-year history. The Giants drew 201,662 fans and earned $45,000 profit for their owners, finally taking the pennant and going on to beat Brooklyn in the World Series, 6-3. Brooklyn switched from the American Association to the National League in 1890, and also took the pennant that year.

Hard drinking was a continuing feature of professional baseball, and ruined several prominent careers. Ed Delahanty, who hit .400 in 1884 and .408 in 1889 and had a lifetime average of .346, was one of the best hitters and hardest drinkers in the National League's early history. He had a .376 average in 1902,

and was playing for the American League's Washington club in 1903 with a .333 average in June when he was suspended for drunkenness in Detroit. On the way home to Washington he was put off the train after a drunken brawl. Delahanty tried to reboard, fell into the river near Fort Erie, Ontario, and was swept over Niagara Falls. His broken body was found a week later.

Two outstanding teams whose exploits are now legendary dominated the National League during the 1890s. The Boston Beaneaters took five pennants, 1891-1893 and 1897-1898, relying on outstanding players for their success, while the 'scientific' style of playing perfected by the Baltimore Orioles under manager Ned Hanlon gave his club three pennants, 1894-1896 (they placed second the next two years), and set the style that was to predominate in the National League until the introduction of the lively ball altered baseball's basic offensive concepts.

The Boston Beaneaters, a strong team during most of the National League's first 25 years, flowered under manager Frank Selee in the 1890s. Selee paid little attention to strategy during the game, but had a remarkable knack for spotting and nurturing talent, his eye proving itself again after he left Boston, when he formed the Chicago team which dominated the National League from 1906 to 1910.

In 1890, Selee brought Charles 'Kid' Nichols up to Boston from the Western League. Nichols, who featured an excellent fastball thrown with good control, proceeded to pitch a decade of games unequalled since pitchers began throwing overhand. From 1890 to 1899 Nichol's win totals were 27, 30, 35, 33, 32, 30, 30, 30, 29, and 21. For the first nine years, he averaged over 30 wins a season. He never fell below

Above: The pennant-winning New York Giants of 1889. Manager James J 'Truthful Jim' Mutrie is in civilian clothes at center.
Far left: Charles Augustus 'Kid' Nichols, the star pitcher of the Boston Beaneaters from 1890 to 1901. He finished his career with Philadelphia in 1906. A Hall of Famer (elected in 1949), he had a lifetime record of 360-202 and an earned run average of 2.94.

20 wins for all ten years, during which he pitched as many as 50 complete games a season, and failed to finish only 22 games. Nichols, elected to the Hall of Fame in 1949, ended his career with 360 wins, the seventh best of all time.

Supporting Nichols on those Boston teams were sluggers Bobby Lowe and Hugh Duffy, pitcher Vic Willis, infielders Fred Tenney and Jimmy Collins, and superstars John Clarkson and 'King' Kelly, both purchased from Chicago for an astounding $10,000 each. Bobby Lowe became the first to set the as yet unsurpassed record of hitting four home runs in a single nine-inning game. Showered with silver coins by his fans, Lowe managed a single his last time at bat. Hugh Duffy also established an all-time record, hitting .438 – the highest ever under modern rules – in 1894. The diminutive Duffy hit over .300 in each of his first ten full seasons in the majors. Of his 236 hits in 1894, 18 were home runs, 15 were triples, and 51 were doubles.

Baltimore finished 12th in the first half of the expanded National League's 1892 split season, but under manager Hanlon, who joined the club on 9 May 1892, the Orioles became one of the greatest collections of ball players ever assembled. Hanlon's lineup included six future Hall of Famers: Dan Brouthers, John J McGraw, Hughey Jennings, Wilbert Robinson, Joe Kelley and 'Wee Willie' Keeler, whose famous prescription for batting success was, 'Keep your eye clear and hit 'em where they ain't.'

The Orioles moved from ten games under .500 (60-70) in 1893 to 50 games over .500 (89-39) in 1894, the first of their pennant years. That season the team batted .343, led the league in fielding and stole 343 bases. Brouthers hit .347, McGraw .340 and the star outfield of Brodie, Keeler and Kelley hit .366, .371 and .393! Even without depth in the pitching staff, such batting talent coupled with Hanlon's strategic skill carried the day. When Hanlon took his methods and a few key players to Brooklyn in 1899, the Brooklyn club took pennants in 1899 and 1900.

Before the 1894 season, Hanlon took his Orioles south for spring training, then an unusual move. At a time when the game consisted entirely of individual effort, Hanlon taught his players to back up bases and each other, and to change position to take cutoff throws, He perfected the hit-and-run play, pioneered by Cap Anson and King Kelly, and used it with devastating effect against the Giants in 1894. His Oriole catchers were also the first to feint throws to trap base runners and to become involved in cutoff plays. What became known as 'inside baseball' was born here, the team working together as a unit. Giant manager John Montgomery Ward exclaimed as they devastated his team, 'That's not baseball they're playing.'

True to the spirit of the age, the Orioles were not cowed by the rules of good sportsmanship. An Oriole base runner would happily skip a base if the umpire turned his back, and an opposing base runner might find third baseman McGraw holding on to his belt long enough to upset his dash for home. Pete Browning once scored by unfastening his belt and leaving it in McGraw's hand. Extra balls hidden by Orioles in the tall outfield grass helped prevent extra bases when a ball was hit beyond the outfielders, and Oriole men planted in the stands substituted mushy balls for balls hit foul by the opposing side. Hanlon instructed his groundskeeper to slope the infield to facilitate bunts.

Oriole basemen didn't hesitate to mutilate opposing base runners. Pittsburgh's great shortstop Honus Wagner recalled how the Orioles limited what should have been a home run to a triple when the first baseman gave him the hip as he rounded the base; the second baseman 'almost killed me, Jennings tripped me at shortstop, and when I got around to third McGraw was waiting for me with a shotgun.'

The Orioles and their fans were no kinder to umpires. According to John A Heydler, an umpire who later became president of the National League, 'They were mean, vicious, ready at any time to maim a rival player or umpire . . . they broke the spirits of some very fine men. I've seen umpires bathe their feet after

McGraw and others spiked them through their shoes ... Other clubs patterned after them, and I feel the lot of the umpire was never worse than in the years when the Orioles were flying high.'

Major-league baseball was not an honorable sport. Winning was important, not how you played the game. Connie Mack, who caught for Pittsburgh in the 1890s, used to mimic the sound of a foul tip with his hands. Sometimes he touched the bat as the batter began his swing, a practice he abandoned when one hitter went for his hand instead of the ball and smashed his fingers.

National League owners played just as rough, especially during the last decade of the century. The country was in a continuing business depression in the 1890s, and clubs such as Chicago, Boston and New York, which had netted annual profits of nearly $100,000 from 1885-1889, never got near those figures. Total National League losses for 1890 were estimated at half a million. In 1898, Boston grossed $50,000, but only five of the league's 12 clubs showed a profit.

Left: Jesse Cale 'The Crab' Burkett, whose lifetime batting average was .340 over his 16 years of playing for New York, Cleveland and St Louis in the National League and St Louis and Boston in the American. He was elected to the Hall of Fame in 1946.

Far left: Cornelius Alexander 'The Tall Tactician' McGillicuddy – better known as Connie Mack – when he played for Pittsburgh from 1891 to 1896. Previously he had been with Washington in the National League and Buffalo in the Players' League. But it was not for his playing (lifetime batting average .247) that he was best known. This former catcher, who was elected to the Hall of Fame in 1937, spent three years as the Pittsburgh manager (1894-1896), then became the manager of the Philadelphia American League club until 1950 – a total managing tenure of 53 years. During that time he won nine pennants and five World Series.

In crushing the American Association, the National League had ended the colorful World Series. The selfish actions of the owners, who now styled themselves 'magnates,' after the captains of industry of the era, alienated fans. Magnate fought magnate, magnates fought players, players fought umpires and league fought league, spewing a wearisome train of lawsuits and slander which taxed the public's patience. Attendance declined.

The most enduring scar etched by the magnates was the so-called 'syndicate' approach to baseball organization. New York Giant owner Andrew Freedman advocated turning the league into a trust, pooling players, franchises and profits under a single organization, shifting players and franchises according to profit opportunities. 'Freedmanism' did not succeed, but it caused serious infighting among the league's clubs, with crippling effects. Baseball pioneer Al Spalding remarked in 1911 that along with gambling and drunkenness, the owners of this era were among the three all-time evils faced by major-league baseball.

It was a National League torn by internal power struggles that refused to recognize the inevitable arrival of a second major league, and chose in 1901 not even to discuss Eastern franchises for Ban Johnson's well-run American League. League war followed. Johnson had little trouble raiding National League players dissatisfied with greedy owners and a league salary ceiling of $2400. In 1901, 111 of the American

League's 182 players came directly from the National League. Among the stars who jumped to the American League and never came back were Wee Willie Keeler, Cy Young, Sam Crawford, Jimmy Collins, Elmer Flick, Ed Delahanty, Nap Lajoie and Jesse Burkett of the St Louis Cardinals, who took the National League batting title in 1901 with a .376 average.

When American League attendance climbed to 2,200,000 in 1902, the National League attendance dropped to 1,683,000 and the National League decided to make peace. Early in 1903 the National Agreement finally gave the Americans major league status, reallocated territorial rights for the 16 major franchises and bound both leagues to a common system of schedules, player contracts and playing regulations (with significant but not major differences).

A National Commission was formed to oversee major league baseball, consisting of the presidents of the two leagues, Harry C Pulliam and Ban Johnson; commissioner-at-large August Herrmann of Cincinnati (reelected each year) and a non-voting secretary. American baseball was to find peace and prosperity for 18 years under the National Commission.

In 1903, with the rules and dimensions of baseball the same as they are today, the National League's eight franchises fixed until 1953, the threat of Freedmanism vanquished, the war with the American League over, and the first Modern World Series, the game entered an era of returning prosperity that marks the beginning of baseball's modern age.

CHAPTER TWO

The
Modern Game

**Oh, it's great to be
young and a Giant.**

Larry Doyle, second baseman for McGraw's Giants

The war with the American League brought many changes in club rosters, forcing a shift in the National League's balance of power away from the clubs that had dominated the 1890s, to three new centers and a new breed of owners and managers who wrote history their own way. Beginning in 1901, the Pittsburgh Pirates, the New York Giants and the Chicago Cubs were to dominate the National League for the next two decades.

The Cardinals, led by Jesse Burkett and Bobby 'Mr Shortstop' Wallace – both of whom jumped to the American League after the 1901 season – topped the league in attendance in 1901, with almost 380,000 paid admissions. By 1906, Wallace, then with the St Louis Browns, was baseball's highest salaried player at $6000 a year. But the best the Cardinals could do in 1901 was fourth, and it was the Pittsburgh Pirates who took the pennant, as they were to do in 1902 and 1903.

Among Pittsburgh's most valuable players during the opening years of the century were pitcher Deacon Phillippe, third baseman Tommy Leach, playing manager Fred Clarke and of course shortstop Honus Wagner. All were acquired as a unit from Louisville after that club left the league in 1899.

John Peter 'Honus' Wagner, indisputably one of the greatest players of all time, was the good-natured, folksy son of a Pennsylvania coal-mining family of German descent. An extraordinarily versatile player, in the 1901 season, before he settled in to set the standard for shortstop, he played 24 games at third and 54 in the outfield, as well as 61 at shortstop. In later years he even pitched on occasion. Big and awkward-looking, he led the National League in stolen bases five times, and his career total of 772 places him fifth in major-league history. His unorthodox, wide-open batting stance earned him a lifetime average of .329 and a league record for most hits (including four consecutive batting titles) that stood until Stan Musial broke it in 1962. But Honus, who was satisfied when he became a $10,000-a-year man and never asked for more, was also capable of playing a strong game according to the ruthless standards of the day. In the 1909 World Series – so legend has it – Ty Cobb, preparing to steal, yelled to Wagner, 'Get ready, Krauthead, I'm coming down.' 'I'll be waiting,' Wagner replied, and tagged Cobb so hard with the ball that he split his lip.

In 1902 Pittsburgh finished 27½ games ahead of second-place Brooklyn, the largest margin by a

Below: Roderick John Wallace, also known as 'Bobby' or 'Rhody,' was another outstanding shortstop. During his 25-year career (1894-1918) he batted .268 while striking out a mere 79 times – 39 of them in his first three years. Wallace, who was elected to the Hall of Fame in 1953, played with Cleveland and St Louis in the National League and St Louis in the American League.

Above: Joe McGinnity (left) talks with John McGraw, his manager on the New York Giants. 'Iron Man' McGinnity pitched for Baltimore and Brooklyn before joining the Giants in 1902. At the end of his career in 1908, he had won 247 games with an ERA of 2.64. He was elected to the Hall of Fame in 1946. 'Little Napoleon' McGraw played baseball for 16 years, but it was as a manager that he was elected to the Hall of Fame in 1937. From 1903 to 1932 he was manager of the New York Giants.

Right: McGinnity (left), McGraw (center) and Christy Mathewson. Christopher 'Big Six' Mathewson pitched for the Giants for 17 years (1900-1916). He was elected to the Hall of Fame in 1936 for his 373-188 record and his 2.13 lifetime ERA.

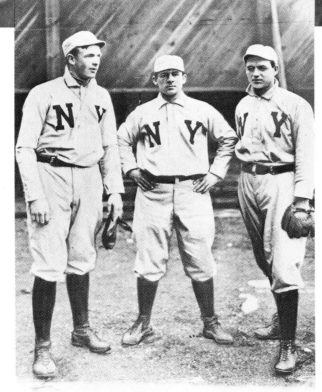

winner in major league history. That year Pittsburgh's Ginger Beaumont led the league in hitting with .357, while Wagner led in stolen bases, runs scored, runs batted in, doubles and slugging average. Tommy Leach was league home run champion with a modest six homers, pitcher Jack Chesbro won 28 games and pitchers Phillippe and Tannehill each won 20. The Pittsburgh pitching staff produced an incredible 130 complete games in 141 starts, winning 103 and losing only 36. Despite the loss of Chesbro, Leach, Tannehill and Conroy to the American League at the end of the season, the club managed to win again in 1903, with Wagner hitting .355 to lead the league and pitchers Phillippe and Sam Leever combining to win 49 games. The Boston Pilgrims took the first American League/National League World Series from the Pirates, 5-3.

A new force had slowly been gathering strength in the National League, and the 1904 and 1905 pennants went to the New York Giants. Under fiery John McGraw, this club was to total ten flags between 1904 and 1924. In 31 years of managing, McGraw's teams added 11 second places to his ten flags, and finished in the first division 27 times. No manager before or since has matched his impact on the game.

In practice, McGraw exercised extremely close

control over his men. Players did almost nothing without his guidance – 'The Little Napoleon' called pitches and gave signals to his batters on every pitch. Tyrannical, brilliant, innovative, 'Muggsy' (a nickname he hated) flamboyantly cursed fans, defied league presidents and was particularly famous for his battles with umpires. As a star player for the great Orioles of the 1890s, McGraw once succeeded in inciting a lynch mob to wait for an umpire after a game with a rope. The umpire wisely waited for the mob to disperse before he left the park. But even those who hated McGraw never questioned his superiority as a manager, and many great players of the era did not consider their careers complete until they had played for him. Second baseman Larry Doyle expressed it best: 'Oh, its great to be young and a Giant.'

In 1902, when McGraw took over the Giants for owner John T Brush, he knew he could not escape the cellar. The Giants finished at the bottom of the league in 1902, as they had in 1900. But McGraw, who had a three-year contract, began drilling his team in the classic deadball style, adding five key men in 1903, and by his first pennant in 1904, he had created the nucleus of a franchise which was to remain the most profitable in the league and in all of major league baseball until the great Yankees teams of the 1920s.

Central to his success was the superb pitching of 'Iron Man' Joe McGinnity and Christy Mathewson. McGinnity topped the 30 mark in 1903 and 1904, but it was Christy Mathewson, acquired by the Giants two years earlier in a trade with Cincinnati for famous pitching great Amos Rusie, one of the titans of the 1890s, who was to supply the key to Giant success until his retirement in 1915.

Even though Mathewson had won 20 games the preceeding season, when McGraw took over stewardship of the Giants in 1902, outgoing manager Horace Fogel was trying to turn him into a first baseman. McGraw, recalling the pitching weakness of his old Oriole clubs and anxious to create a strong pitching staff, put Mathewson back on the mound. Despite the disparities in their personalities and backgrounds, Mathewson and McGraw were to become lifelong friends, and always roomed together on the road.

At a time when most players came from poverty-ridden childhoods, Mathewson, son of a gentleman farmer and a wealthy mother, educated at Keystone Academy and Bucknell (where he was class president and member of the glee club and literary society), supplied a new standard for the baseball idol. Tall, good-looking and literate, a non-drinker who seldom smoked and opposed Sunday baseball (a continuing controversy), he was also a fierce competitor, with uncanny control over the fastball, breaking curve and fadeaway (or screwball), a pitch he pioneered. Both as a player with 373 lifetime wins and as a sportsman he was admired by his peers, and this handsome Adonis was the first baseball player to be held up as an example to young boys. His reputation was so spotless, in fact, that his wife sometimes went out of her way to remind the public that he could swear and had not yet sprouted wings.

Christy Mathewson demonstrates his windup. He became the manager of the Cincinnati club in 1916, staying on until 1918. Unfortunately, his managerial record (.482) did not compare to his pitching record.

Beginning in 1903, with 30 wins, Mathewson won 30 or more games for three straight years – a feat matched by only four other pitchers in the history of the game – and 20 or more for 12 consecutive years. In one stretch of five years he allowed less than 2 earned runs per game each season, and he five times led the league in wins, ERA's, and strikeouts. In 1904, he added 33 wins to McGinnity's 35 as the Giants swept to victory 13 games ahead of the second-place Chicago Cubs, setting a new major-league record of 106 wins. McGraw's jackrabbits also stole a total of 283 bases that year.

Due to a long-standing feud with American League President Johnson, Brush and McGraw refused to meet the American League winner in a 1904 World Series, claiming, 'There is nothing in the constitution or the playing rules of the National League which requires the victorious club to submit its championship honors to a contest with a victorious club in a minor league.' Hoping to prevent further interrup-

Far right: Roger Philip 'The Duke of Tralee' Bresnahan, the Hall of Fame (elected in 1945) catcher. His career spanned 17 years, from 1897 to 1915, and he played for Washington, Chicago, New York and St Louis in the National League and Baltimore in the American League. He also managed the Cardinals from 1909 to 1912, but finished in the first division only once – coming in fourth in 1915.
Below: Joe McGinnity warms up.

tions in the popular postseason playoffs, the National Commission moved over the winter to institutionalize the world championship, and the World Series rapidly captured public interest to become the capstone of the baseball season it remains today.

Mathewson rose to national stardom in the 1905 World Series when he pitched three shutouts against the Philadelphia Athletics (McGinnity pitched one, too) as the Giants took the Series after winning a hard-fought pennant from Pittsburgh. Mathewson won 31 games that season and lost only eight, with a 1.27 ERA. He was to pitch even greater seasons before moving on to manage Cincinnati and become president of the Boston Braves, but lungs weakened by poison gas in World War I interrupted his postwar career time and time again, and he died of tuberculosis in 1925 at the age of 45.

Spurred on by a pitching staff that was exceptional even in an era dominated by tight pitching, the Chicago Cubs took four pennants between 1906 and 1910, coming in second with 104 games in 1909. They set a National League record with an average of 106 wins a season for these five years, and a still-standing major-league record of 116 wins in 1906.

Heading the staff of playing manager Frank Chance's pitching aces was Mordecai 'Three Finger' Brown, who with Mathewson was the outstanding National League pitcher of the century's first decade. A childhood accident with farm machinery had cost Brown half his right index finger and mangled two others, but enabled him to throw a baffling, unnaturally sharp breaking ball. Pitching for the Cubs in 1906, Brown was 26-6, with a 1.04 ERA. Jack Pfeister was 20-8, Ed Reulbach 19-4 and Carl Lundgren 17-6, for a team ERA of 1.76. Chicago's team batting average that year was .262, topping a league with five teams batting under .241. Despite the brutal pitching, Pittsburgh's Honus Wagner hit .339 to take his fourth league batting championship.

The next year, Chicago, winning 107 games, finished 17 games ahead of second-place Pittsburgh. Wagner again took the National League batting championship with a .350 average, the Pirates leading the league with a .254 team average, 11 points above the league average. But it was still a pitcher's game. Aided by an outstanding infield and continued excellent pitching

by Brown, Orval Overall, and Reulbach, Chicago recorded a team ERA of 1.73, the lowest in National League history. On 18 May, National League President Pulliam announced that the league was finally out of debt after seven years in the red.

The Chicago club of this dynasty featured the famous infield of Tinker, Evers and Chance, immortalized by columnist Franklin P Adams in a verse which first appeared in a July 1910 edition of the *New York Mail*. Third baseman Harry Steinfeldt, who hit .327 and led the league with 83 RBI's in 1906, should also be mentioned in this memorable infield, which included playing manager Frank Chance on first, Johnny Evers on second and Joe Tinker at shortstop. While the legendary trio was highly efficient, by all accounts they were far from being the era's best infield or its most adept practitioners of the double play. This defensive combination, in fact, only became a familiar play a decade later when the introduction of the lively ball made for more sharply hit balls and faster fielding. More than anything else, the enduring legendary status of this trio illustrates the power of the pen in an age when the game's only medium was the newspaper, and sportswriters could make or break a reputation.

The Cubs took their third straight flag in 1908, but only after a hard-fought battle with the Giants and Pittsburgh that ended in one of baseball's most controversial moments. On 23 September 1908, the Cubs met the Giants at the Polo Grounds for a game which

Above: Johnny Evers (left), the second baseman, and Joe Tinker, the shortstop, of the Chicago Cubs' famous double play combination – Tinker to Evers to (Frank) Chance. Evers – 'The Trojan,' 'The Cat' – played for Chicago for 11 of his 18 years, finishing with a .334 career average. He also managed both Chicago teams. Joseph Bert Tinker's career extended from 1902 to 1916, beginning and ending with the Cubs. Both were elected to the Hall of Fame in 1946.
Far left: Mordecai Peter Centenniel Brown, also known as 'Three Finger' Brown and 'Miner,' began his pitching career with St Louis in 1903. The next year he went to the Cubs, where he stayed until 1912. He then went to Cincinnati, Brooklyn and Chicago of the Federal League, and returned to the Cubs in 1916 – his last year. He was elected to the Hall of Fame in 1949 because of his 239-130 record and his 2.06 ERA.

Above: The Polo Grounds at Coogan's Bluff in New York in 1905.
Right: Frank Chance, the first baseman in Chicago's Tinker to Evers to Chance double play combination. Frank Leroy Chance – 'Husk' or 'The Peerless Leader' – joined the Cubs as an outfielder/catcher in 1898, but by 1903 he was their regular first baseman, and stayed there until 1913, when he joined the Yankees for his last two seasons. From 1905 to 1914, he was the player-manager of his club, winning four pennants and two World Series with the Cubs. He was inducted into the Hall of Fame in 1946 – the same year that his two teammates made it.

could have decided the pennant. With two men out and the score tied 1-1 at the bottom of the ninth, the Giants got men on first and third. Giant shortstop Al Bridwell hit a single to center, and the man on third came home for the winning run. Technically, the man on first, 19-year-old Fred Merkle, should have tagged second before heading for the clubhouse, but he didn't. This was common practice at the time, and Merkle did nothing that any other player wouldn't have done. However, Cub second baseman Johnny Evers got the ball (or a ball) and touched second, turning Bridwell's hit into a forceout at second.

That was how umpire Hank O'Day called it. That meant that the run Bridwell hit in was nullified, and the game was still tied and should go into extra innings. But jubilant Giant fans were already swarming the field, certain their team had won, and with darkness descending, umpire O'Day called the game and declared it a tie.

League President Pulliam upheld the umpire's ruling, and the Giants and the Cubs finished the season with identical records. Despite the protests of both clubs, a playoff was scheduled. Three Finger Brown took the game 4-2 from Christy Mathewson, who otherwise had his greatest season with 37 wins and a 1.43 ERA, and the Cubs went on to take the Series from Detroit. Fred Merkle, although stoutly defended by McGraw, lived out the remainder of a fine 16-year career in the majors under a cloud, forever known as 'Bonehead,' hounded by a press which chose to hold him personally responsible for performing according to common practice. President Pulliam's suicide less than a year later was motivated

But McGraw's Giants came back to dominate the league for three years, taking the pennant in 1911, 1912 and 1913. During those years Mathewson's wins totaled 26, 23 and 25; and lefthander Rube Marquard, known as the '$11,000 Lemon' after his purchase from Indianapolis in 1908 until he hit his stride, took 24, 26 and 23, including 19 consecutive games in 1912. In the course of taking the 1911 pennant, the Giants stole 347 bases, still the major-league record.

The Giants lineup of those years was generally set with Fred Merkle, Larry Doyle, Art Fletcher and Buck Herzog in the infield; Chief Meyers behind the plate and Red Murray, Fred Snodgrass, Josh Devore and George Burns in the outfield. The team was drilled to perfection in McGraw's system, receptive to his signalled commands. Often a player was bullied by McGraw until he shaped up and responded automatically to a given situation. The way the Giants fired the ball around the bases when they were warming up let the opposition know that McGraw and his team were all business on the ball field.

1911 saw more effects of the cork-center ball, with the Cub's Frank 'Wildfire' Schulte hitting 21 homers to break the previous major-league record of 16. Chief Meyers hit .332 (he hit .358 in 1912, the league record for a catcher) as the National League batting average climbed to .260.

Mathewson, Three Finger Brown, and Brooklyn's Nap Rucker continued to be the league's top pitchers, but only Mathewson had an ERA of less than 2.00 (1.99). The real news in pitching that year came from the Phillies' Grover Cleveland Alexander, who set a still-standing rookie record of 28 wins, 7 shutouts and 227 strikeouts. Alexander was destined to become one of the greatest pitchers of all time, matching Christy Mathewson's National League record win total of 373 games.

1912 featured the incredible year of Chicago's third baseman Heinie Zimmerman. He led the league with 207 hits, including 14 home runs and 42 doubles, for a batting average of .372, but missed the Chalmers Award, that era's equivalent of the Most Valuable Player Award, a Chalmers automobile bestowed by the Chalmers Company. During the four-year life of the award, 1911-1914, its recipients were Wildfire Schulte, Larry Doyle, Jake Daubert and Johnny Evers, who in 1914 was playing for the 'miracle' Boston Braves.

No pennant or World Series race since 1914 ever passes without some reference to the 'Miracle Braves' of 1914. On 19 July 1914 the Braves were in last place, but after an incredible winning streak, by 10 August they had climbed to second place, 6½ games behind McGraw's Giants. They moved into first place on 2 September, slipped briefly to third, and returned to first on 8 September. After winning 60 of their last 76 games, they took the pennant by 10½ games over the Giants, the first time a club other than the Giants, Cubs or Pirates had taken a National League pennant since 1900.

Braves manager George Stallings announced early in the season, 'I have 16 pitchers, all of them rotten,' but it was Dick Rudolph's 27-10, Bill James's 26-7 and George Tyler's 16-14 hurling that carried the Braves to the title. Walter 'Rabbit' Maranville at shortstop and Johnny Evers at second base supplied excellent infield support. The Philadelphia Athletics were universally expected to put the upstart Braves in their place in the World Series, but instead became the first team to be counted out in four games as the Braves pulled their second major upset of the year. During

in part, it was believed, by the criticism he received for upholding the umpires.

1908 marked the high point of the pitchers' dominance, with the hurlers holding the batters to a .239 average, still the lowest in National League history. Honus Wagner, however, managed to take another batting title, hitting .354, and the next year helped his club win 110 games and the pennant to celebrate owner Barney Dreyfuss's new triple-decked steel ballpark, Forbes Field, with a capacity of 25,000. Wagner hit .333 in the World Series, which the Pirates took from the Tigers in seven games.

The Cubs returned to the winner's circle in 1910, 13 games ahead of the Giants, with essentially the same team that had been successful in 1906. Batting averages rose by 12 points over the preceding year and the hit-and-run play began to replace the sacrifice bunt as a somewhat livelier cork-center baseball patented by A J Reach became available for major-league play. 1910 also saw President Taft toss out the first baseball at the Washington season opener, beginning a practice that developed into a tradition, and of course it was in July of 1910 that Franklin P Adams wrote:

These are the saddest of possible words
– Tinker to Evers to Chance
Trio of Bear Cubs and fleeter than birds
– Tinker to Evers to Chance.
Thoughtlessly pricking our gonfalon bubble,
Making a Giant hit into a double,
Words that are weighty with nothing but trouble –
– Tinker to Evers to Chance.

the Series pitchers James and Rudolph both won two games each. Hank Gowdy batted .545, and Chalmers Award winner Evers, who seemingly willed the Braves to victory, hit .438.

In 1914, with the beginning of the war in Europe, the National League faced a war of its own. The Federal League, boasting such affluent backers as Chicago's James A Gilmore, oil tycoon Harry Sinclair and Brooklyn baking barons the Ward Brothers, began raiding players, and made plans to move from minor to major-league status for the coming season. For its franchises in Chicago, St Louis, Pittsburgh, Kansas City, Brooklyn, Buffalo, Newark and Baltimore, the Federal League purchased such National League stars as Joe Tinker, Three Finger Brown, Howie Camnitz, Claude Hendrix, Ed Reulbach, Tom Seaton – who won 27 games for the Phillies in 1913 – and Lee Magee.

Although the Federal League was never financially successful, it went to plenty of trouble and caused considerable losses. Some estimates for combined league losses run as high as $10 million. Hoping to see something for its efforts anyway, the Federal League tried to have the entire structure of organized ball invalidated in court by suing the majors for violating the Sherman Anti-Trust Law. Owner Sinclair applied additional pressure by announcing plans to move his Newark club to New York City, where it would be in direct competition with established major-league clubs.

Judge Kenesaw Mountain Landis, the federal judge who heard the case, took the summer to consider the anti-trust suit, hoping to avoid making a decision, and eventually the National League opted to negotiate. The Federal League agreed to disband, and in return, the National League awarded $400,000 to the Wards, $100,000 to Sinclair, permitted the Federal League's Charles Weigham to buy the Cubs, and arranged for buy-backs of National League contract-jumpers, and for the sale of Federal League players. The war, at great cost, was over.

In 1915, with Christy Mathewson pitching 8-14 and

about to move on to managing the Cincinnati Reds, Grover Cleveland Alexander became the league's leading pitcher, etching a 31-10 record with twelve shutouts. His 1.22 ERA remained a league record until Bob Gibson broke it in 1968, and was an accomplishment all the more remarkable because half of his games were pitched in the tiny bandbox of Baker Bowl. Alexander was ably abetted in hurling the Phillies to their first National League pennant by outfielder Gavvy Cravath, one of baseball's greatest home run hitters, who tagged 24 homers to break Wildfire Schulte's record of 21. But league batting honors went to Giant second baseman Larry Doyle, with a .320 average, the lowest ever for a title in the league. John McGraw, for the first and only time in his New York managerial career, finished in the cellar, an embarrassment somewhat mitigated by a record which left the Giants only 3½ games behind the fourth-place Cubs.

The Brooklyn Dodgers took the pennant in 1916, becoming the third National League team in a row to earn its first pennant. In those days the Dodgers were known as the Robins, after portly manager Wilbert Robinson, a lovable bumbler and walking sideshow who had played behind the plate on the legendary Orioles teams of the 1890s. Probably the most popular figure in Brooklyn baseball history, 'Uncle Robbie' drew crowds to impressive new Ebbets Field, now in its fourth season, with his clownish antics, but it was his skill in developing pitchers that won him the pennant.

In 1916, Robin hurler Ed Pfeffer won 25 games to lead a pitching staff that included Marquard and Jack Coombs. Slugging power was supplied by Zack Wheat, Jake Daubert and Casey Stengel. Ex-Giants Merkle and Meyers, in addition to Marquard, also played for the Dodgers that year, a fact which added fuel to persisting rumors that the Giants helped their former teammates beat out the Phillies for the pennant by dropping a crucial series to the Robins. At one point during a Robins-Giant game at Ebbets Field, McGraw himself stalked off the field calling his men

'quitters,' and yelled to the press box, 'I'll be no part of this.' An investigation proved inconclusive, and the Robins finished 2½ games ahead of the Phillies. Despite a spectacular 26-game winning streak in September, the Giants finished fourth behind Boston.

Grover Cleveland Alexander posted another extraordinary season with 33 wins, including an all-time record of 16 shutouts, 9 of them in tiny Baker Bowl. Also beginning to be heard from was the Cardinals' Rogers Hornsby, still dividing his time between third base and shortstop, who hit .313 in his first full season.

Two years after dropping such aging stars as Christy Mathewson and rebuilding, McGraw's Giants took the pennant in 1917. Newcomers Ferdie Schupp on the mound and hitters George Burns and Benny Kauff were instrumental in New York's 98 wins, two years after the club had finished at the bottom of the league. Despite his talented youngsters, McGraw lost his fourth consecutive World Series, this time to the White Sox. For delivering an uppercut to the jaw of umpire Bill Byron, however, McGraw received a $500 fine and a 16-day suspension. When he continued the fight by attacking league President Tener and the umpires in the press, he was fined another $1000.

Although the Phillies finished 10 games behind the Giants, Grover Alexander again dominated league pitching with a 30-13 record, his third consecutive 30-game season. Pittsburgh's Honus Wagner retired at the age of 43 with a record of 3430 hits that stood for 45 years.

On 2 May 1917, Fred Toney of the Reds and Jim 'Hippo' Vaughan of the Cubs engaged in the only

Top: An early flag-raising at Ebbets Field. The Dodgers of the period had reason to look glum.
Right: Fred Toney, who pitched for Chicago, Cincinnati, New York and St Louis in a career that went from 1911 to 1923.

double no-hitter in major-league history. During the first nine innings, each pitcher issued only two bases on balls. In the top of the tenth inning, Vaughan gave up two hits and the Reds scored one run. Toney then retired the Cubs in order, maintaining his no-hitter through the tenth inning.

A few days before the 1917 season began, Congress declared war on the Central Powers of Europe. Hank Gowdy of the Braves was the first major-leaguer to enlist, but it was not until the next season that baseball, classified as a non-essential industry, began to feel the heat. General Enoch Crowder's June 'Work or Fight' order forced all draft men to choose between the military and essential industries. By the 11 November 1918 Armistice, a total of 103 National Leaguers had entered the service, including Christy Mathewson, Branch Rickey, Casey Stengel, Rabbit Maranville, Rube Benton, Ed Pfeffer, Eppa Rixey, Bill James, Eddie Grant (killed near Verdun) and Grover Cleveland Alexander. At Secretary of War Newton Baker's suggestion, the season was shortened to end on Labor Day, 2 September. As attendance declined, the owners panicked. In 1918 Giant owner Harry Hempstead sold out to Charles Stoneham. Fearing Alexander's conscription, the Phillies had sold him to the Cubs for two players and $60,000 the previous

Below: Edd J 'Eddie' Roush began in the outfield with the White Sox in 1913. He then played one year with Indianapolis and one year with Newark in the Federal League, winding up with Cincinnati in 1917. In 1927 he went to the Giants and ended his career back in Cincinnati in 1931. His .323 lifetime batting average helped him into the Hall of Fame in 1962.

November, a shortsighted move that helped plunge the Phillies into the cellar for years to come.

The war-shortened season was the first in which runner-up clubs were given an incentive to continue playing their best in the final weeks of the season. The practice of allocating a share of the World Series receipts to first division clubs, devised by league President Tener, has continued ever since. The Cubs took the pennant that year, led by Hippo Vaughan's 22 wins.

Under the constant shelling of trench warfare, Grover Cleveland Alexander lost his hearing in one ear and developed epilepsy. Although, like many players of the era he was a heavy drinker, after the war his drinking increased to epic proportions, largely, it is now supposed, as a mask for his problems. At the time alcoholism was more socially acceptable than epilepsy, and it now seems likely that much of his erratic behavior, attributed to drink, was actually due to his illness. Alexander was never to return to his previous heights of achievement, but it is a tribute to his extraordinary natural ability that he remained an effective pitcher after the war, and three times won at least 21 games in the hit-happy 1920s.

The National League, uncertain what the postwar economy would bring, reduced its playing schedule from 154 to 140 games in 1919, but was pleasantly surprised to find baseball enthusiasm reaching new heights everywhere.

The Cincinnati Reds, led by slugger Edd Roush, won their first pennant in 1919, finishing 9 games ahead of the second-place Giants, and went on to upset the Chicago White Sox in the World Series, 5-3. (From 1919-21, the World Series was extended to require five wins instead of four.) The White Sox, unquestionably one of the greatest teams of all time, were hands-down favorites to take the Series, and many felt that their performance was suspiciously substandard. A year later it was determined that eight White Sox players had conspired with gamblers to throw the Series.

By then the National Commission, under fire and losing effectiveness for the last five years, had been dissolved and had been replaced by a single commissioner, Judge Kenesaw Mountain Landis, who was given a seven-year contract at $50,000 annually. Serving until 1944, when he was 78, Landis was given sweeping, dictatorial powers, and charged with cleaning up the game. Nothing else, it was felt, would restore public confidence.

Landis's first major ruling was to banish the eight Chicago players responsible for throwing the 1919 World Series. The eight, who were eventually acquitted by a Chicago grand jury, were Eddie Cicotte, Claude Williams, Chick Gandil, Swede Risberg, Buck Weaver, Joe Jackson, Happy Felsh and Fred McMullin. Landis also barred Chase, Zimmerman and Magee. The message got through to players and fans alike.

With the postwar economy booming and confidence and enthusiasm in the game assured by the presence of Landis and the exploits of Babe Ruth, the beginning of the Roaring Twenties marked a turning point as baseball and the National League entered a period of unprecedented prosperity. New York legalized Sunday baseball in 1920, and rule changes were introduced to handicap pitchers, encourage hitters, and make the game more exciting and popular with fans.

Both leagues outlawed all trick pitches that involved tampering, such as the application of sandpaper, emery, or saliva to the surface of the ball,

although 17 pitchers in the majors who used the spitball as their primary weapon were permitted to continue to do so. In the National League this included Bill Doak, Phil Douglas and Burleigh Grimes, the last legal spitballer, who pitched in the majors until 1934. For the first time since the early days, when batters could call for their pitchers, hitters were favored over pitchers.

But the introduction of the lively ball was probably even more significant. Despite repeated assurances by such National League officials as President Heydler that the only change in the manufacture of the ball was more firmly-bound better quality wool yarn, a baseball officialdom bent on wooing fans after the Black Sox Scandal could not have helped but notice that more home runs and higher-scoring games drew more spectators to the park. From 1918 through 1920, league home run totals climbed from 138 to 261.

In 1921, they shot up to 460; and in 1930, the figure was 892. Officials still claim the ball is the same as it has always been, but it is difficult to reconcile the 1930 National League batting average of .303 (after the 1930 season the ball was made *less* lively) with the knowledge that only six batters in the National League hit above .300 in 1968.

In 1920, spurred on by spitballer Burleigh Grimes's 23 wins and the hitting of veteran Zack Wheat, Wilbert Robinson's Brooklyn Dodgers took their second pennant, finishing seven games ahead of the second-place Giants. McGraw managed to squeeze 20-game seasons from hurlers Jesse Barnes, Art Nehf and Fred Toney as the league returned to the prewar 154-game schedule.

An amazing pitching duel took place on 1 May 1920 between Brooklyn's Leon Cadore and Boston's Joe Oeschger. With both pitchers going all the way, their game was called for darkness at 1-1, but only after 26 complete innings had been pitched. The names of both pitchers in this longest-ever game in baseball history, neither of whom gave up a run after the sixth inning, remain forever fixed in baseball legend.

The Phillies's Cy Williams led the league in home runs with 15 that year (Babe Ruth hit 54, more than any National League team except the Phillies), but the real hitting news in the National League was Rogers Hornsby's .370 batting average. Although modest by his later standards, it was good enough to earn him the first of six consecutive league batting championships. He was to take seven in all. Hornsby's 1920 average of .370 was followed by averages of .397, .401, .384, .424 (still the major-league record) and .403. On

President Warren G. Harding throws out the first ball in Washington, DC, to open the 1922 baseball season – 12 April 1922.

Above: Leon Joseph Cadore pitched for the Dodgers (1915-1923), and ended his career with a lifetime ERA of 3.14.

Right: Joe Oeschger was a mainstay pitcher for several clubs from 1914 to 1925.

the way to earning the league record lifetime batting average of .358, 'The Rajah' led the league twice in homers (his 42 homers and 154 RBI's in 1922 set new league records), four times in doubles, five times in runs scored, four times in RBI's, and nine times in slugging. Hornsby's lifetime slugging percentage of .557 is still a record for the National League.

In 1920, Hornsby led the league not only in batting average, but in slugging, RBI's, doubles and hits. This was also the year in which he was permanently switched to second base, a position he played with excellence. The Rajah was such a fanatic about his hitting that he refused to attend movies or to read much beyond the racing form for fear it might damage his eyes. Without a weakness at the plate and impossible to pitch to, in 1924, when he hit .424, he was walked so often that he got on base more than 50 percent of the time he came to bat.

But if Rogers Hornsby was the greatest all-round hitter in National League history, he was also one of the most arrogant and tactless men in a game not known for refined etiquette. His record of playing for five different teams and managing five different teams is directly attributable to the inability of any owner, manager or player to put up with his 'frankness,' even when he was winning.

In January 1921, the owners of both leagues signed a new National Agreement binding players, umpires, and owners to Commissioner Landis's decisions, and empowering him to levy fines of up to $5000. In baseball matters, the owners even waived their rights to seek justice in civil courts. Should Landis die without a successor being chosen, the President of the United States was to appoint his replacement. Judge Landis again proved he could crack the whip by ordering the Giants's Charles Stoneham and John McGraw to sell their racetrack, club, and casino in Havana or get out of baseball.

McGraw stayed in baseball and completed his current team-building by buying Johnny Rawlings, Emil 'Irish' Meusel and Casey Stengel from the Phillies. The Giants went on to take the pennant, the first of four consecutive flags the club was to take in this decade of hitters, making it the first in major league history to take four consecutive pennants. The unstoppable Giant teams which swept the flags from 1921-1924 featured Frankie Frisch, Art Nehf, Travis Jackson, Dave Bancroft, George Kelly, Ross Youngs, Frank Snyder and Hack Wilson. These were McGraw's greatest teams. Art Nehf, Fred Toney, and the rest of the pitching staff were decent but never great – only Nehf managed a 20-game season during the four

Right: Rogers 'Rajah' Hornsby, was elected to the Hall of Fame in 1942. Primarily a second baseman, he played between 1915 and 1933 for the Cardinals, Giants, Braves, Cubs and the Browns in the American League. He had a lifetime batting average of .358 and managed – from the 1920s to the 1950s – the Cardinals, Braves, Cubs, Browns and the Reds, winning the 1926 World Series with the Cardinals.

Left: Ross Youngs played the outfield for the New York Giants from 1917 to 1926, and was elected to the Hall of Fame in 1972. His career batting average was .322.

Far left: Henry Knight 'Heinie' Groh had a long career at second and third base with the Giants, the Reds and Pittsburgh, and managed Cincinnati in 1918.

pennant years – and it was Giant sluggers who gave the club its power. In 1924, Heinie Groh, with an average of .284, had the lowest average in the starting lineup.

Giants Ross Youngs and Frank Frisch particularly stood out for their drive and energy. Youngs, nicknamed 'Pep,' was a favorite of McGraw's, but his brilliant career was cut short by a kidney disease which caused his death in 1927. In McGraw's later years, the only pictures on his office walls were of Ross Youngs and Christy Mathewson.

Frisch, a speedy infielder with even more fire than Youngs, was ranked by many of his contemporaries as the finest National League player of the era. Like Honus Wagner, the versatile and competitive Frisch was always the first pick for any All-Star team. He and his manager respected each other's skill, but Frisch's sharp tongue and intolerance of criticism didn't mix well with McGraw's authoritarian manner, and eventually the two could no longer stand to share the same clubhouse. When McGraw traded Frisch after the 1926 season, it was for none other than Rogers Hornsby, the highest paid National League player, earning $42,000 a year as the playing manager for the Cardinals.

The Giants finished the 1921 season four games ahead of the second-place Pirates. Meeting the Yankees in the Polo Grounds, they lost the first two games, won the second two, lost the fifth to the Yankees, and then took three in a row to clinch the Series. This was the first time a Series winner had lost the first two games, and the first Series played in one park.

With pitchers struggling to adapt to the lively ball,

Far right: Philips Brooks 'Shufflin' Phil' Douglas near the end of his career. He pitched for the White Sox in 1912, moved to the Reds in 1914, played for the Reds, the Dodgers and the Cubs in 1915, stayed with the Cubs until he went to the Giants in the middle of the 1919 season, and remained there until his retirement in 1922. While his record was a paltry 93-93, he ended up with a 2.80 ERA.
Below: Frankie Frisch practicing his head-first slide. Frank Francis 'The Fordham Flash' Frisch, elected to the Hall of Fame in 1947, had a fabulous career with the Giants (1919-1926) and the Cardinals (1927-1937). This second baseman ended his 19 years with a .316 batting average and 2880 hits. He also managed the Cardinals (1933-38), the Pirates (1940-46) and the Cubs (1949-51), winning the pennant and the World Series with St Louis in 1934.

ERA's and batting averages rose steadily. The fans responded to the hitters' game by pushing attendance up throughout the league. In 1927, the Chicago club became the first in National League history to host over one million paying customers. In 1922, the year the Supreme Court ruled that baseball was not subject to Sherman Anti-Trust laws, the league batting average was .292, with the Pirates batting .308 as a team. The Giants finished the season seven games in front of Cincinnati, and once again faced the Yankees in the World Series, which had returned to a best-of-seven match at the suggestion of Commissioner Landis.

The Giants took the Yankees in four games and one tie, but the season was marred by an unfortunate incident involving Giant pitcher Phil Douglas, who wrote a drunken letter to Leslie Mann of the Cardinals in which he offered to 'go fishing' for the rest of the season, for a good price, to help the Cardinals take the pennant. Douglas's offer was undoubtedly in reaction to what must have been an excessively humiliating public chewing out by manager McGraw. He later called Mann and asked him to destroy the letter, but Mann had already shown it to Cardinal manager Branch Rickey, who showed it to Landis, and the Commissioner banished him from the game forever.

The Giants took the 1924 pennant 4½ games ahead of the second-place Reds, but dropped the World Series to the Yankees, 4-2. In 1924 McGraw's men took what was to be his tenth and final flag, finishing 1½ games ahead of Brooklyn, but not without another unfortunate scandal. Before the 27 September game, Giant Jimmy O'Connell offered Phillies shortstop Heinie Sand $500 if he would not 'bear down too hard.' Sand refused the offer, told his manager, and the affair eventually reached Landis.

O'Connell, a promising young outfielder for whose minor league contract the Giants had paid $75,000, testified that he thought all the Giants knew about the bribe offer and that he had only approached Sand because Giant coach Cozy Dolan had told him to. O'Connell particularly implicated Giant stars Frisch, Kelly and Youngs. These three were exonerated, but Dolan's plea of lapse of memory infuriated the Commissioner, who banished O'Connell and the coach from organized ball forever. There was speculation that the whole affair had been an elaborate practical joke played on the gullible O'Connell. The Giants went on to lose the World Series to Washington in the seventh game.

In 1924, the league inaugurated the Most Valuable Player Award. A committee of writers selected Brooklyn pitcher Dazzy Vance, with a 28-6 record, over Rogers Hornsby, who had batted an indelible .424 for the Cardinals. That same year Cardinals first baseman Jim Bottomley established a major league record by driving in 12 runs, with 6 hits, in a single game.

In a decade in which hitters terrorized pitchers, Brooklyn's Dazzy Vance proved it was still possible to strike batters out. The Dodger pitcher, who didn't land permanently in the majors until 1922, when he was 31, led the league in strikeouts from 1922-1928. In his MVP year of 1924 he also led the league in wins, complete games and ERA. His 262 strikeouts in 1922 were achieved in a year in which no other pitcher in the league struck out more than 86, with the exception of spitballing teammate Burleigh Grimes, who fanned 134.

As the National League began its 50th season, the Pirates moved up from their third-place berth in 1924

James Joseph 'Jimmy' O'Connell played for the New York Giants for two years, 1923-24. This outfielder batted .270.

Above: Clarence Arthur 'Dazzy' Vance pitched for 16 years in the majors and was elected to the Hall of Fame in 1955. He started in Pittsburgh in 1915 and went to the Yankees that same year. In 1922 he began his tenure with the Dodgers, leaving for the Cardinals in 1933. He was traded to the Reds in 1934, but returned to the Cardinals that same year. He ended his career with the Dodgers in 1935, with a lifetime 3.24 ERA.
Far right: Harold Joseph 'Pie' Traynor spent his whole career (1920-1937) with the Pittsburgh Pirates. This third baseman had a lifetime batting average of .320 and accumulated 2416 hits.

to take the pennant and end the Giants' four-year reign. The key to their finish 8½ games ahead of McGraw's club was a preseason raid engineered by owner Barney Dreyfuss which brought George Grantham, Vic Aldridge and Al Nichaus to Pittsburgh. Hurler Aldridge won 15 games, and Grantham hit .326 to help compile a team average of .307. Although Johnny Morrison, Emile Yde, Lee Meadows and Ray Kremer also contributed solid pitching, it was Pirate hitting which propelled them to the top.

Pie Traynor, on his way to becoming baseball's all-time third baseman, hit .320; Glenn Wright, the shortstop who made an unassisted triple play that season and formed an airtight left side with Traynor, hit .308; Earl Smith hit .313; Kiki Cuyler hit .357; Max Carey hit .343 and Clyde Barnhart hit .325. In a World Series in which Max Carey hit .458 and Kremer and Aldridge both won two games each, the Pirates finally beat the Senators in the seventh game. On opening day of the Series, Christy Mathewson died of tuberculosis at Saranac Lake.

Rogers Hornsby, batting .403 and taking his second Triple Crown, was selected as 1925's Most Valuable

Until then, most minor-league clubs were independently owned, selling their better players to the big leagues. Rickey's idea was for the Cardinals to buy and run their own farm clubs. Beginning in 1919 with the acquisition of part interest in the Houston club, the Cardinal farm system eventually extended to include 50 teams with more than 800 players under contract. Rickey's eye for talent was legendary, his priority was on speed, and his method proved effective. After the Cardinals paid $10,000 for Jess Haines in 1919, more than 25 years passed before the club purchased another established star. The great St Louis teams of the intervening years were all the products of Rickey's farm system.

The first crop of Rickey's farmers made their mark in 1926, under manager Hornsby. But even in 1943 and 1946, when the Cards took pennants after Rickey was long gone from the organization, the winning teams were still primarily his farm products. By then the farm system had become standard operating procedure for nearly every club in the majors.

Grover Cleveland Alexander, war-scarred and 39, also contributed to the Cardinals' pennant of 1926. After being traded in the middle of the season from

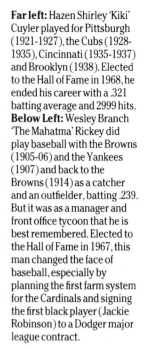

Far left: Hazen Shirley 'Kiki' Cuyler played for Pittsburgh (1921-1927), the Cubs (1928-1935), Cincinnati (1935-1937) and Brooklyn (1938). Elected to the Hall of Fame in 1968, he ended his career with a .321 batting average and 2999 hits.
Below Left: Wesley Branch 'The Mahatma' Rickey did play baseball with the Browns (1905-06) and the Yankees (1907) and back to the Browns (1914) as a catcher and an outfielder, batting .239. But it was as a manager and front office tycoon that he is best remembered. Elected to the Hall of Fame in 1967, this man changed the face of baseball, especially by planning the first farm system for the Cardinals and signing the first black player (Jackie Robinson) to a Dodger major league contract.

Player. In the middle of the season he took over management of the St Louis Cardinals, bringing them in fourth, and in 1926, Hornsby's first and last full season as their manager, the Cardinals took their first modern pennant. Every team in the National League had now won at least one flag.

The last St Louis pennant had been the Brown's win in 1888. Beginning in 1926, the Cardinals were to become a major force in the league, winning nine flags and six World Series over the next two decades. Their greatness during this period was unquestionably the result of the policies of general manager Branch Rickey, one of the finest intellects ever to come into the game and properly known as the father of the farm system, who joined the impoverished Cardinals in 1919 and hit upon a brilliant idea to make his team a contender in a league in which rich clubs could insure their success by outbidding poorer clubs for star players. 'Let's grow our own talent,' he suggested to owner Sam Breadon, 'we can round up promising young prospects and develop them on our own minor-league clubs.'

Below: The great St Louis Cardinal team of 1926 that beat the Yankees four games to three in the World Series. Grover Cleveland Alexander is in the front row, far right.

the Cubs, who thought he was burnt out, he won nine games. In one of the most dramatic World Series of all times, Alexander, emerging from the bullpen with a legendary hangover in the seventh inning of the seventh game, Cardinals leading 3-2, struck out Tony Lazzeri with bases loaded, and pitched two more hitless innings. He had already won the second and the sixth games. After the Series, winning manager Rogers Hornsby was traded to the Giants for Frank Frisch.

The 1927 pennant went to a Pittsburgh club with a .305 team average. Finishing only 1½ games ahead of the Cardinals, the Pirates featured the hitting of the Waner brothers, Paul and Lloyd, who got more than 5600 hits between them, and so terrorized National League pitchers in the 1920s and 1930s that they became known as Big Poison and Little Poison. In 1927, Paul Waner, in his second season with the Pirates, led the league with a .380 average. Younger brother Lloyd, in his rookie year, hit .355, the two brothers totalling 460 hits toward that year's Pirate pennant.

The Giants, finishing two games behind the Pirates, now featured Hornsby at second base. Hornsby, who hit .361, assumed his duties only after forcing league owners to buy back Cardinal stock he had bought at $45 a share, insisting he be paid $116 a share. Star Giant outfielder Ross Youngs sat out the season with Bright's disease and died on 22 October. The Cardinals were obliterated in four games in the World Series by a Yankee team regarded by many as the best team of all time.

Frustrating McGraw's hopes for an eleventh pennant by two games, the Cardinals, with Frisch on second base, returned to the winner's circle in 1928, clinching the pennant on the next-to-last-day of the season. Chick Hafey, a product of the St Louis farm system and one of the finest National League outfielders ever, hit .337, while teammate Jim Bottomley

Far right: Frankie Frisch warms up.
Below: The Waners with the Pirates – Lloyd and Paul (center and right). Lloyd James 'Little Poison' Waner played the outfield for Pittsburgh from 1927 to 1941. In 1941 he went to the Braves and then to the Phillies. In 1945, his last year, he returned to the Pirates. Elected to the Hall of Fame in 1967, he was a lifetime .316 hitter. Paul Glee 'Big Poison' Waner also played the outfield in Pittsburgh, starting in 1926. In 1941 he was traded to Brooklyn and then to Boston. He returned to Brooklyn in 1943, went to the Giants in 1944, and finished his career with the Yankees in 1945. Elected to the Hall of Fame in 1952, he carried a batting average of .333.

led the league in RBI's with 136, hitting .325, and tying Chicago's Hack Wilson for home runs with 31. Rogers Hornsby took his seventh and last league title with an average of .387. He was playing for the Braves in 1928. Apparently one season had been all McGraw could stand of the outspoken slugger.

With Babe Ruth hitting .625 and clouting three home runs in one game of the World Series and Lou Gehrig racking up four homers and a .545 Series average, the Cardinals, like the Pirates of the year before, went down before the awesome Yankees in four games. John Heydler, elected league president for another four years, suggested a way to speed up the game and promote interest by substituting a pinch-hitter for the pitcher. The pitcher would stay in the game, but the pinch-hitter would handle his at-bats. In 1973 the idea of the Designated-Hitter was finally adopted by the American League.

Under the stewardship of former minor-league infielder Joe McCarthy, the Cubs beat out the second-place Pirates by 10½ games in 1929, the first of nine pennants for manager McCarthy and the first flag since 1918 for the Cubs. As more and more life was pumped into the ball, batting averages continued to swell and balls flew out of the parks. The Cubs' winning outfield of Kiki Cuyler, Hack Wilson and Riggs

Stephenson batted .360, .345 and .362, respectively. Rogers Hornsby, now on second base for the Cubs, traded the previous November for five players and $200,000, hit 40 homers, 149 RBI's and racked up a .380 average, for which he received his second MVP Award. At the summer meeting the league directors decided to discontinue the award, now in its seventh year.

Philadelphia's Lefty O'Doul took the league title with an average of .398 on a team which averaged .309 overall. His teammate Chuck Klein averaged .356, taking the league home run title with 43. Both Klein's homers and O'Doul's 254 hits were new National League records. While most of the tumbling league records involved slugging, Grover Cleveland Alexander, in the last game he ever won, equalled Christy Mathewson's lifetime mark of 373 wins.

55,980 baseballs were used that year in the National League, topping the previous year's total by 4644, a figure that would have been greater without the new screens erected above the outfield walls at the St Louis and Philadelphia parks. Even so, the National League hit a new record of 754 home runs – an increase of 144 over 1928 – and would have hit more if the umpires hadn't started rubbing the gloss from the balls before the game at mid-season. But the exploits of the sluggers of 1929 was only a prelude to what was to come in 1930.

Left: Chick Hafey stretches for a high one. For 13 years (1924-1937) Hafey played the outfield with the Cardinals and the Reds, carrying a batting average of .317. He was elected to the Hall of Fame in 1971.
Far left: Lefty O'Doul takes a swing. O'Doul played for the Yankees from 1919 to 1922, then for a succession of teams, but ended his career in 1934 with the Yankees, hitting, .349.

CHAPTER THREE

The League
Takes to the Air

Brooklyn?
Is Brooklyn still in the League?

Bill Terry

In 1930, with the nation in economic crisis, 5.5 million paying customers visited National League ball parks, half a million more than the previous year, setting a new league record. Brooklyn topped the million mark for the first time, and the Cubs set a home attendance record with 1,463,264.

If the National League managed to escape the immediate effects of the Depression, it was probably because the owners, exploiting the fans' enthusiastic reaction to the hitting game, pumped more life into the ball than ever before. As a result, new records were set all season, some of which may never be matched. Six clubs – the Giants, Phillies, Cardinals, Cubs, Dodgers and Pirates – posted team batting averages of over .300. By comparison, in 1968 only six players in the National League hit .300 or better.

Leading the pack in individual hitting was Chicago's stubby, hard-drinking outfielder Lewis 'Hack' Wilson with 190 RBI's – a major-league record – and 56 home runs – a National League record that still stands. Only Hank Greenberg, with 183 RBI's in 1937, has ever remotely approached Hack's 190 RBI's. Wilson was originally with the Giants in 1923, but a clerical error exposed him to the draft, enabling the Cubs to grab him for next to nothing in 1925.

The Giants led the league with a collective average of .319. Giant second baseman Bill Terry, in the midst of ten straight seasons of batting over .300, led the league with 254 hits and a season average of .401. His lifetime average of .341 makes him second in modern National League history only to Rogers Hornsby, and first for left-handed hitters. Terry and Lefty O'Doul, who got 254 hits in 1929, still hold the major-league record for hits. In 1930, Terry became the last National Leaguer to hit .400.

The Phillies, averaging .315 as a team, featured Lefty O'Doul with a .383 average, and Hall of Famer Chuck Klein, who hit .386, including 250 hits, 59 doubles, 40 home runs, 170 RBI's and 158 runs scored. Incredible as it may seem, in this year of the hitter only Klein's doubles were a new record, and his team, with a pitching staff ERA of 6.71, finished a dismal last, 40 games out of first place.

In the National League in 1930, 11 players hit better than .350 and 17 players drove in more than 100 runs. Babe Herman of the Dodgers hit .393 and Fred Lindstrom of the Giants hit .379. With averages of .330-.340 commonplace, ERA's rose correspondingly. The last-place Phillies yielded 7.7 runs per game; Brooklyn, in fourth, had an ERA of 4.03, due largely to the pitching of Dazzy Vance, now 39, who led the

Below: Hack Wilson hits a long fly at Wrigley Field – 1930. Lewis Robert Wilson played the outfield for the Giants (1923-25), the Cubs (1926-31), the Dodgers (1932-34) and the Phillies (1934). In his 12-year career, he batted in 1062 runs and hit .307.

Above: 'Dizzy' Dean, the young Cardinal super-pitcher.

Left: Johnny Leonard Roosevelt 'Pepper' Martin – 'The Wild Hoss of the Osage' – in the St Louis dugout. Martin played the outfield and third base for the Cardinals for 13 years – 1928 to 1944 – and hit .418 in the three World Series he was in.

league with an ERA of 2.61. His closest competition was New York's Carl Hubbell, with 3.76. The league as a whole averaged an ERA of almost five runs per game.

The Cardinals, featuring eight .300 hitters in their lineup and four more on the bench, finished two games ahead of the Cubs to take the pennant. Once the flag was secure, they broke ground by starting 19-year-old Jerome Dean – also known as Jerome Herman and Jay Hanna – in the last game of the season. Known to the world as Dizzy Dean, the young righthander won his game in nine innings, allowing one run and three hits. The Cardinals dropped the World Series to the Athletics, 4-2.

As the Depression deepened, attendance declined with the nation's financial health. Total baseball receipts of $17 million in 1929 declined steadily to a low of $10.8 in 1933, before climbing slowly to $21.5 million in 1939, followed by a wartime slump, and a new height of $68.1 million in 1948. But during the hard years, baseball provided the public with a chance to at least temporarily forget the harsh realities of its economic winter. At the 1931 World Series, Cardinals *vs* Athletics, President Herbert Hoover's

Members of the St Louis
Cardinals Gas House Gang
clowning before a game.

presence was greeted with boos, while Cardinal rookie Pepper Martin, following up a .302 rookie year with 5 stolen bases, 12 hits and a .500 Series average, was greeted with tumultuous applause and screams of appreciation.

Johnnie Leonard 'Pepper' Martin, also known as the 'Wild Hoss of the Osage' after the Oklahoma farm country in which he was born, was a product of the Cardinal farm system. An uninhibited natural man who used his chest to slide on or to block hot grounders and for years saved expense money by hopping a freight train south to spring training – both practices giving him his characteristically filthy appearance – Pepper was the perfect antidote for the Depression blues.

He was also the perfect addition to a club which soon came to be known as the 'Gashouse Gang,' one of the best-remembered clubs in league history and the most colorful club since the old Orioles. But even with Pepper spearheading the Cardinals to a 1931 pennant finish 13 games ahead of the Giants and a sensational World Series win, St Louis attendance dipped from 623,960 in 1931 to 290,370 in 1932, bottoming out at 268,404 in 1933. When the Cardinals won the pennant in 1928, they had drawn 778,147 fans.

After the 1930 season, evidently even the owners realized that their formula for success had been

mixed a little too rich, and over the winter they squeezed some of the juice out of the ball. Not surprisingly, batting averages declined dramatically in 1931. The league average of .277 for 1931 was 26 points off the preceeding year.

1931 witnessed the closest batting race in history, with the Cardinals' Chick Hafey eventually emerging as league leader with a .3489 average after edging out Bill Terry's .3486 and teammate Jim Bottomley's .3482. Scoring high in the booze league, Hack Wilson hit an unremarkable 13 home runs and 129 fewer RBI's than his record of the previous year. The Cubs led the league with a team average of .289, 30 points less than the Giant's record of 1930. Notable events of the season included the forced retirement of the Dodgers' 'Uncle Robbie,' Wilbert Robinson, manager since 1914, and the refusal of the league directors to reestablish the Most Valuable Player Award. The MVP was taken over by the Baseball Writers Association of America, who awarded it to Frank Frisch.

Beginning a year of surprising managerial moves, in 1932 the Giants' John McGraw followed former Oriole teammate Robinson out of the game, ending one of the longest and most colorful careers in baseball. Strangely enough, only one sportswriter was there to report the event. On 3 June 1932, Tom Meany of the *World Telegram* stopped by the Giant clubhouse looking for a story. A doubleheader with the Phillies had been rained out, and the clubhouse was empty, but he found a notice on the bulletin board announcing that John McGraw had resigned as manager of the Giants and had been succeeded by Bill Terry.

At 59, worn out and ailing – he would die of uremia within two years – McGraw's departure was less of a shock than his choice of Bill Terry to succeed him. Terry was outstanding among a growing number of players who would not put up with McGraw's authoritarian style. The two had barely spoken for years, and most observers felt that brilliant Giant third baseman Fred Lindstrom was McGraw's clear choice, as did Lindstrom, who later asserted he had been lied to. Yet when faced with the task of picking a successor, McGraw rose above personal differences to pick the man he felt was best suited for the job.

Cubs manager Rogers Hornsby was fired with the Cubs in first place on 2 August 1932 after a series of vitriolic policy disputes with club president William Veeck. Charlie Grimm replaced him, and the Cubs went on to take the pennant four games ahead of Pittsburgh, then demonstrated their opinion of Hornsby by not voting him any share in the World Series money.

Below: John McGraw, perhaps the greatest manager in baseball. John Joseph 'Little Napoleon' McGraw played both infield and outfield for Baltimore in the American Association (1891), Baltimore in the National League (1892-99), the Cardinals (1900), Baltimore in the American League (1901-02) and the Giants (1902-06). He hit .344, but is best remembered for his managerial genius. He headed Baltimore in the National League (1899), Baltimore in the American League (1901-02) and the Giants (1902-32), winning nine pennants and three World Series with New York. McGraw was elected to the Hall of Fame in 1937.

Among the notable rookies who came up that year were Brooklyn pitcher Van Lingle Mungo, Chicago second baseman Billy Herman, and Pirate shortstop Arky Vaughan, who was to carve a place for himself as shortstop second only to the great Honus Wagner. The Cardinals, who never rose above fourth place and ended up in a sixth place tie with the Giants, distinguished themselves by adding Joe Medwick and Dizzy Dean to their regular lineup. Called up from Houston at the end of the Texas League season, Medwick batted .349 in 26 games. Dean, pitching 18-15 in his first full season, led the league in strikeouts with 191, as well as in shutouts and innings pitched.

The son of an Arkansas sharecropper, Dizzy Dean, one of baseball's all-time purveyors of joy and a pitcher of uncanny natural ability, succeeded in replacing the fading Babe Ruth as the game's greatest draw. Throughout the Depression his fractured English, homespun personality and amazing antics, both calculated and natural – and unlike many, Dean was no drinker – delighted the American public. He sometimes predicted shutouts and other pitching feats in advance, maintaining that it wasn't bragging if he went out and did it after saying it. On one occasion, after he had pitched a three-hitter in the first game of a doubleheader and his brother Paul pitched a no-hitter in the second game, the Great One remarked, 'If I'd known Paul was going to do that, I'd have pitched a no-hitter too.'

His practical jokes made him undisputed king of the Gashouse Gang, which featured such equally irrepressible personalities as Pepper Martin, short-

– perhaps the best the league has ever seen – was coupled with a control so remarkable that he walked fewer than two men per game in 16 years in the majors.

Chuck Klein of the Phillies was the league's top hitter of 1933, taking the Triple Crown with 28 home runs, 120 RBI's and a batting average of .368. The previous year the Baseball Writers had voted him MVP on the strength of 38 homers, 137 RBI's and a batting average of .348. As a reward, after the 1933 season the Phillies sold him to the Cubs for three players and $65,000. Throughout the decade the Phillies, desperately in need of cash, developed and sold star players.

In the World Series, the Giants beat the Washington Senators, who they had faced at their last Series appearance in 1924, in five games. Mel Ott, the Giant slugger whose 511 home runs were the National League record until Giant Willie Mays broke it, hit two homers and batted .389 for the Series.

Branch Rickey's farm system continued to pay off in 1934 as the Cardinals, managed by Frank Frisch, finished two games ahead of Bill Terry's Giants to take their fifth pennant in nine years. With the fiery Frisch at the helm, the Gashouse Gang (so named when lippy Leo Durocher commented to a sportswriter the year before that the American League would probably call them 'a bunch of gashouse players'), flowered with a spirit achieved by only a handful of clubs in the history of the game. Dizzy Dean pitched his greatest

Left center: Paul Dean (left) and his brother Dizzy – both outstanding pitchers. Paul Lee 'Daffy' Dean played for St Louis from 1934 to 1939 (from 1934 to 1937 the two brothers were the mainstays of the Cardinal pitching staff), then for the Giants and the Browns in the American League. Although he had a 3.75 ERA, he never lived up to the potential he showed during his first two seasons in which he won 19 games each year.

stop Leo Durocher and Joe Medwick. On one afternoon, Dizzy gave three separate interviews to three different sportswriters, claiming a different birthplace in each interview. He later explained that he wanted each writer to have his own story. Dizzy Dean was only one of three or four names he went by anyway.

In their first full season under Bill Terry, the Giants, who finished sixth in 1932, moved into the lead on 10 June 1933 and led all the way, finishing 5 games ahead of the Pirates. Pittsburgh outhit the Giants .285 to .263, but Giant pitching, with Hal Schumacher taking 19, Fred Fitzsimmons 16 and Carl Hubbell 23, made all the difference.

This was the year that Carl Hubbell – henceforth known as 'Meal Ticket' – came into his own, hurling 10 shutouts (including 46 consecutive innings of shutout pitching), and leading the league with a 1.66 ERA, the best in the National League since Alexander's 1.22 in 1915. Hubbell pitched the finest game of his career on 2 July 1933, shutting out the Cardinals 1-0 in 18 innings. In the All-Star game, starting against an American League lineup all of whom became Hall of Famers, Hubbell struck out in order Babe Ruth, Lou Gehrig, Jimmie Foxx, Al Simmons and Joe Cronin, and kept the Americans scoreless for the three innings he pitched under All-Star rules.

In 1933 Hubbell began a string of 5 consecutive years in which he won at least 21 games, averaging 23, with a high of 26 in 1936. Quiet, thoughtful, and publicity-shy, he was in every way the antithesis of his arch-rival Dizzy Dean. Hubbell's notorious screwball

Left: Carl Hubbell warms up. Carl Owen ('King Carl,' 'The Meal Ticket') Hubbell pitched for the Giants from 1928 to 1943, winning 253 games with an earned run average of 2.97. He was elected to the Hall of Fame in 1947.

Chuck Klein receiving his 1932 Most Valuable Player trophy. Charles Herbert Klein roamed the outfield for 17 years with the Phillies (1928-33), the Cubs (1934-36), the Phillies again (1936-39), the Pirates (1939) and the Phillies again (1939-44). He hit 300 home runs and carried a .320 batting average.

season, becoming the first National League pitcher to win 30 games since Grover Cleveland Alexander in 1917, and leading the league with 24 complete games, 195 strikeouts and seven shutouts. In true down-to-the-wire Gashouse style, his 30th win and seventh shutout came on the last day of the season, and also clinched the pennant.

At the start of the season, Dizzy had predicted that he and his brother Paul, who came up to the Cardinals through the farm system, would win 45 games. But Paul, quiet and soft-spoken – nicknamed 'Daffy' nevertheless – won 19 games, for a combined total of 49.

Joe 'Ducky' Medwick, on his way to establishing

himself as the best National League hitter of the 1930s, backed up his club's pitchers with 106 RBI's and a .319 average. At the World Series, Medwick got into an altercation with Detroit third baseman Marv Owen which resulted in such violent demonstrations of vegetable throwing by the Detroit fans that Commissioner Landis removed him from the game as a safety precaution. The Cardinals won anyway, after Dizzy Dean told the Detroit manager that his starting pitcher on the seventh game would 'never do,' and went on to win by striking out star hitter Hank Greenberg in the bottom of the ninth with two men on and two men out.

This was the year when Giant manager Bill Terry, asked for his pre-season evaluation of various National League clubs, remarked, 'Brooklyn? Is Brooklyn still in the League?' Terry was not given to public wisecracks, and he lived to regret this one. The Dodgers, sometimes known as the 'Daffiness Boys' after a term Westbrook Pegler coined almost a decade earlier, had fallen on hard times indeed, and Terry's quip, because it was so close to home, infuriated the fans.

As fate would have it, with the Giants and the Cardinals tied for first place, the Giants' last two games of the season were against the Dodgers, and the Dodgers, whose fans carried placards with the hated words and greeted Terry with deafening boos every time he made an appearance, won both games. The Cardinals won both of their final games from the last-place Reds, and the Giants were kept from the pennant. McGraw had died on 25 February 1934. Perhaps it was only fitting that the Giants should be disappointed in the year of the passing of their greatest manager by the manager he had chosen to succeed him.

In the 60th year of the National League, baseball tradition was shattered when the Phillies met the Reds at Crosley Field to play the first major-league night game. On 24 May 1935, Franklin D Roosevelt himself pushed a button that turned on 632 lights in a park filled with 20,422 fans, almost ten times the number who would have attended an afternoon contest. Night games are so important to baseball now that it is hard to believe that almost everyone except Cincinnati's dynamic Larry MacPhail opposed them, even though they had already proved successful in the minors. After prolonged negotiations, almost as if to humor MacPhail, each National League team had agreed to play one night game against Cincinnati that season. But once the Depression-hungry clubs evaluated attendance figures at night games, all opposition ceased. Within 13 years, every major-league club except the Cubs had installed lights.

The champion St Louis Cardinals of 1934, who beat the Tigers four games to three in the World Series. Left to right standing – Medwick, Gonzales, Crawford, Whitehead, Mooney, Martin, Vance, P Dean, Frisch, Haines, Hallahan, Durocher, Rothrock, J Dean, Pippen. Left to right seated – Haley, Walker, DeLancy, Orsatti, Carleton, Fullis, Davis, Collins, Wares.

The Hall of Fame has little room for baseball executives, but as front-office men go, the brilliant, irrepressible Larry MacPhail was an undisputed star. In three years with the Reds and five with Brooklyn, he single-handedly pioneered the use of night games as well as of radio, two innovations which changed the face of baseball forever. After taking over the Reds in 1934, his Rickey-like tactics and foresight built the Cincinnati club from a team which hadn't finished better than fourth since 1926 into one which took pennants in 1939 and 1940. After his first year, attendance in Cincinnati doubled.

The challenge he faced in Brooklyn was even greater, but his methods were just as successful. Before MacPhail arrived, the Dodgers had averaged about 500,000 spectators a year. In his first year, they drew 666,000, and in his second, with the club now in third place and their games broadcast on radio, attendance rose to 955,000. Among his many innovations, MacPhail was the first to use motion pictures systematically so that players could study and improve their game.

Babe Ruth came to the Boston Braves in 1935, the year the Braves lost 115 games, the record for the

Far right: Larry MacPhail at the radio microphone.
Below: The first major league night game – Crosley Field, Cincinnati, 24 May 1935.

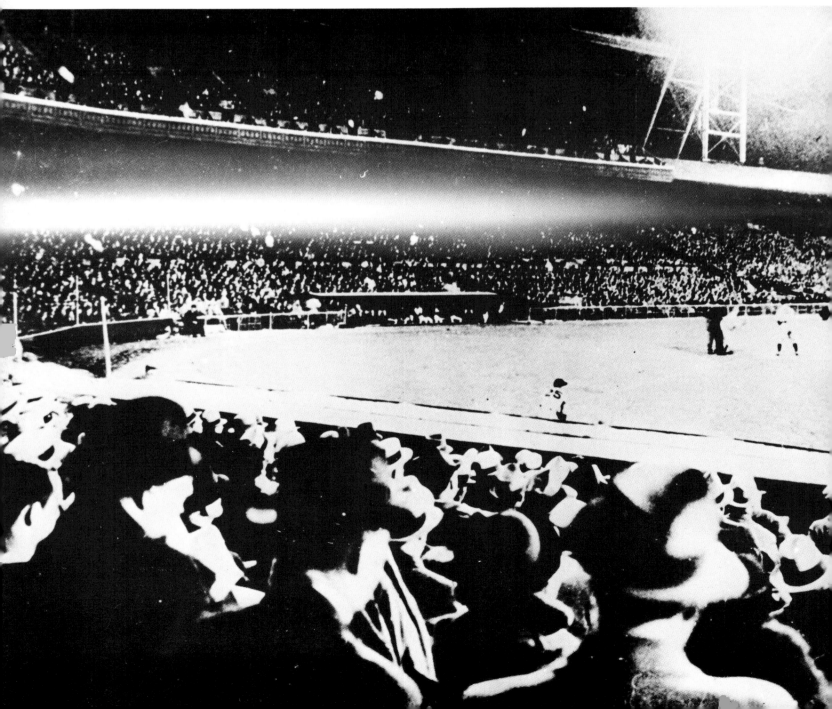

154-game schedule. Ruth batted only .181 for 28 games before retiring on 2 June, but not before hitting three homers on 25 May at Forbes Field, the 712th, 713th and 714th of his career. He never got another hit.

The Giants and the Cardinals ran a close pennant race that year, the Giants leading most of the way until the Cubs took the lead and the pennant with a historic 21-game winning streak in September. Chicago pitchers Bill Lee and Lon Warneke were both 20-game winners, and second baseman Billy Herman hit .341. Dizzy Dean threw 28-12 for the Cardinals while teammate Joe Medwick accrued a .353 average, but top league batting honors that year went to Pittsburgh's Arky Vaughan. His .385 average remains the highest average ever for a National League shortstop.

The great Casey Stengel contributed an anecdote to the archives after his Dodgers, in a display of exquisite bumbling, ended a four-game winning streak by dropping a doubleheader to the Cubs. As the Brooklyn manager climbed into a Chicago barber chair, he announced, 'A shave please, but don't cut my throat. I may want to do it myself later.'

The Giants came back to take pennants in 1936 and 1937. Outfielder Mel Ott, a quiet man with an unorthodox batting style and a special knack for hitting down the Polo Grounds' short right field line, led the league in homers both years, with 33 and 31, but it was Meal Ticket Carl Hubbell who really smoothed the way.

1936 was Hubbell's greatest year. The great screwballer registered a 26-6 record, and closed out the season with 16 consecutive wins. Voted Most Valuable Player, on his way to a 22-8 record in 1937,

Right: Mel Ott stretches for the ball. 'Master Melvin' Ott played the outfield, second and third base for the Giants from 1926 to 1947. Elected to the Hall of Fame in 1951, he had a .304 lifetime batting average.

Hubbell won eight more games in a row, amassing a total of 24 consecutive wins before he was stopped by the Dodgers on Memorial Day. In 1937, rookie lefthander Cliff Melton helped with the pitching chores by adding another 20 games to the Giants' wins.

Above: Arky Vaughn at the plate. Joseph Floyd Vaughn played shortstop, and later the outfield and third base for the Pirates (1932-41) and the Dodgers (1942-48). His lifetime batting average was .318.

On 10 July, Chuck Klein, back with the Phillies after a season with the Cubs, tied the major-league record by hitting four home runs in a single game against Pittsburgh, and a long ball he hit in the second inning which backed Paul Waner against the right field fence almost made it five. After finishing five games ahead of the Cubs and the Cardinals, the Giants lost the Series to the Yankees, 4-2. In the first Hall of Fame election, Honus Wagner and Christy Mathewson were among the first six chosen for the new shrine in Cooperstown, New York.

1937 proved to be Joe Medwick's greatest year. He took the Triple Crown, was voted MVP, and led the league in eight batting categories: average (.374), RBI's (154), home runs (31), runs (111), slugging (.641), at-bats (633), hits (237) and doubles (56). This was the second straight year Medwick led in doubles. The 64 two-baggers he hit in 1936 still stand as a National League record. Cardinal teammate Johnny Mize, another product of the Cardinal farm system, whose lifetime slugging average is second only to Rogers Hornsby's in the National League, turned in a .364 average, hit 25 home runs and 113 RBI's.

In a tragic accident, Cardinal pitcher Dizzy Dean, now 26, sustained an injury that resulted in an incalculable loss to his team and the league. In the third inning of the July 1937 All-Star Game, Dean, who was the starting pitcher for the National League, was hit in the right foot by a line drive off the bat of Cleveland's Earl Averill. The ball broke his toe. Dean returned to action too soon, and in favoring the painful foot he changed his pitching motion, placing an unnatural strain on his arm which eventually ruined it. He managed a 13-10 record that season, but for all practical purposes his career was over. Even so, star deal-maker Branch Rickey was able to unload him to the Cubs the next spring for $185,000 and three players, including the highly competent righthander Curt Davis.

Bill McKechnie, managing in Boston, produced two rookie pitchers who won 20 games each. Neither Jim Turner nor Lou Fette ever won more than 14 games after that, but McKechnie was named *Sporting News* Major League Manager of the Year for 1937 for his masterful stewardship of a mediocre team. In the World Series, the Giants lost to the Yankees again, Carl Hubbell pitching the Giants' only win, 7-3 in the fourth game.

In 1938, the Phillies, now playing in the Athletics' Shibe Park, were granted permission to play under the lights for the coming season, becoming the third National League club with a night schedule. Cautious

Red Barber, the dean of baseball commentators, who broadcast games for the Dodgers and the Yankees.

as the owners had been about night games, their conservatism was nothing compared to their opposition to and fear of radio broadcasts. While Cincinnati had broadcast some games when MacPhail was with the club, until the very end of the 1930s no club broadcast games on a daily schedule, and the only broadcasts that there had ever been out of New York were of World Series and All-Star games.

But as the 1930s progressed, largely at the prodding of Larry MacPhail, broadcasts on the new but well-entrenched medium of radio gradually became the commonplace thing they are today. Far from hurting attendance, as the owners had every right to fear they would, by the end of the decade it became clear that the enthusiasm generated by announcers such as Red Barber created fans. Newspaper sales gained as listeners bought more papers in order to follow game statistics. The revenue radio broadcast brought was particularly welcome during the Depression. In 1933,

Boston earned a modest $5000 from broadcasts. By 1936, Commissioner Landis was able to negotiate $100,000 for World Series broadcasting rights, and the Cardinals, who profited least in the league from radio, were receiving $33,000, while the Giants, who topped the National League in radio revenue, received $100,000 a year for the broadcasts of their games. Altogether, in 1939 National League clubs earned $410,000 in radio money. It is true that major league broadcasts did eventually hurt the minor leagues, but by the time this effect was felt, major league subsidization of the minors was common practice.

1938 will always be remembered as the year that Johnny Vander Meer pitched two no-hitters back-to-back, an unprecedented achievement that remains unequalled. The 23-year-old Cincinnati lefthander, known for speed but also for wildness, was finally brought somewhat under control by Reds manager McKechnie, and on 11 June he pitched a hitless 3-0 victory over the Boston Bees, walking three but allow-

Below: Al Lopez when he caught for the Boston Bees. From 1928 to 1947 Alfonso Raymond Lopez played for the Dodgers, the Bees (as the Braves were known for a time), the Pirates and the Cleveland Indians. But he was better known as a manager – of the Indians (1951-56) and the Chicago White Sox (1957-69), where he won one pennant with each club. He was elected to the Hall of Fame in 1977.

Right: Ebbets Field, 15 June 1938 – Johnny Vander Meer of the Reds beats the Dodgers 6-0 with a no-hitter.

ing no runner to reach second base. With only 20 no-hitters pitched in the league since 1901, Vander Meer's game was a solid achievement.

On 15 June, Cincinnati met the Dodgers at Ebbets Field for Brooklyn's first night game ever. Larry MacPhail, by now running the Dodgers, had arranged pre-game festivities in honor of this historic occasion, including track exhibitions by Olympic champion Jesse Owens and an appearance by Babe Ruth, whom MacPhail had signed as a Dodger coach. Before 38,748 fans, Vander Meer started for the Reds, and although he walked eight men, he kept the Dodgers hitless inning after inning, while the Reds scored four runs in the third. With one out in the ninth, Vander Meer walked three men on 18 pitches, loading the bases, but McKechnie walked out to the mound to calm him down, and Vandy forced Ernie Koy out on a grounder and stopped Leo Durocher with a fly to the outfield, winning his second no-hitter, 6-3.

Vander Meer's no-hit streak eventually ended after 21½ innings on 19 June, when Debs Garms singled against him at Boston. With 15 wins for the 1938 season and a 119-121 lifetime total, Vander Meer's record no-hitters, which are apparently destined to stand for some time yet to come, illuminate an otherwise unspectacular career.

A classic pennant race drama that ended in a famous home run took place late in September when the Cubs met the Pirates in Wrigley Field for a three-day series to decide the championship. The Pirates enjoyed a 1½ game lead before leaving for Chicago, but in the opening game the sore-armed Dizzy Dean beat them 2-1. The next day's game was still tied at the bottom of the ninth. With darkness gathering, it seemed likely the game would be called a tie and

Vander Meer warms up. John Samuel Vander Meer, also known as 'The Dutch Master' or 'Double No-Hit,' pitched for the Reds (1937-49), the Cubs (1950) and the Cleveland Indians (1951). He won 119 and lost 121 with a 3.44 earned run average, but his greatest feat was pitching those back-to-back no-hitters.

Far right: Gabby Hartnett – for 20 years the catcher for the Cubs. A .297 hitter with 236 home runs, Hartnett also managed the Cubs from 1938 to 1940. He was elected to the Hall of Fame in 1955.

Below: Bucky Walters warms up. William Henry Walters pitched for the Boston Braves (1931-32), the Boston Red Sox (1933-34), the Phillies (1935-38), the Reds (1938-48) and then went back to the Braves for the 1950 season. He also managed the Reds in 1948 and 1949, coming in seventh both years. He was 198-160 in his career and had an earned run average of 2.79.

replayed as part of a doubleheader the next day. With two out, the Cubs' Gabby Hartnett, manager since July, came up to bat. After two strikes in the fading light he connected on a fast ball from Mace Brown to hit his immortal 'homer in the gloamin',' winning the game. Now half a game up, the Cubs trounced the dispirited Pirates the next day 10-1, to win the pennant again as they had in 1935, 1932 and 1929, on a weird three-year schedule. The Yankees devoured them in the Series, four straight.

Demonstrating the effects of Larry MacPhail's team-building after he was long gone, and aided by the acquisition of Bill Werber from the Athletics, Bill McKechnie's Cincinnati Reds took the pennant in 1939. Their first flag since 1919, this same team, which finished in the cellar in 1937, would take the flag again in 1940. Werber, an honor graduate of Duke University, proved to be the key to tightening up the Cincinnati infield, and the Reds took the lead with a 12-game winning streak in May which included two victories over the second-place Cardinals.

Righthanders Bucky Walters and Paul Derringer threw 27-11 and 25-7 for the Reds that season. Several of his managers had noticed that Walters, who came to the majors as an infielder, sometimes had so much on the ball when he threw to first base that the first baseman had trouble handling it, but he wasn't converted to pitching until 1935 when Phillies manager Jimmie Wilson, a former catcher, talked him into

it. Even so, Walters didn't think much of the idea, and made the switch mostly to please his respected manager. Traded to the Reds as a pitcher in 1938, Walters followed his 27 wins in 1939 with 22 in 1940.

First baseman Frank McCormick and catcher Ernie Lombardi supplied Cincinnati's hitting. Starting as a regular in 1938, McCormick led the league in hitting in his first three years, averaging .327, .332 and .309. In 1938, Lombardi, with a .342 average, became the second catcher in major-league history to win a batting title. Big and slow-moving, Lombardi's powerful line drives forced the left side of the infield to move back on the grass when he came to bat, a safe strategy

Left: Paul Derringer warms up. Derringer, also known as 'Duke' or 'Oom Paul,' pitched for the Cardinals (1931-33), the Reds (1933-42) and the Cubs (1943-45). The winner of 223 games, he had an ERA of 3.46.

because it took him so long to get to first. Lombardi is remembered for being knocked out in the World Series when Charley 'King Kong' Keller ran into him. Keller was driven in on a single by Joe DiMaggio, who also scored while Lombardi was taking his snooze. The Yankees took the Series from the Reds in four games.

Although the Giants finished in fifth place in 1939, the club set a new record when five of its players hit home runs in one inning of a 17-3 victory over the Reds. The Giant sluggers in the 6 June game were: Harry Danning, Frank Demaree, Burgess Whitehead, Manny Salvo and Joe Moore.

On 12 June, league officials and 10,000 fans celebrated the supposed centennial of baseball at Cooperstown, New York, erroneously believed to be the birthplace of the game.

Commissioner Landis presided over the dedication of the Hall of Fame and Museum, an event which was attended by 10 of the 11 living players so far elected to baseball immortality.

CHAPTER FOUR

Innovation and Upheaval

Nice guys finish last.

Leo Durocher

No decade since the 1880s has brought so many changes to baseball and the National League as the 1940s. After climbing steadily out of the pit of the Depression, organized baseball was totally disrupted by America's entry into World War II in December 1941, just at the point when something like normal prosperity had returned to the major leagues. Neither the country, the world nor the game would ever be the same.

Loss of manpower to conscription and wartime travel and materials restrictions were only part of the story. Within the span of a decade, the National League also had to deal with the player-raiding tactics of the Mexican League, the near-organization of a player's union, and the opening of the game to blacks and Hispanics. In the late 1940s, the advent of television and commercial air travel made it possible for clubs to consider new locations and created the potential for the franchise shifts which would soon become a reality. Night games and radio continued to be a growing force in a decade of astounding social and technological change, all contributing to a period of major upheaval for the National League.

The 1940s will always be remembered as a decade dominated in the National League by two great clubs. From 1941 to 1949, the Cardinals and the Dodgers won seven pennants, stepping aside only for Chicago in 1945 and Boston in 1948. In both those years, the Cardinals came in second. St Louis won four pennants during this period, won the World Series three times and finished second five times. Brooklyn won three pennants and finished second three times.

The opening year of the decade went to the Cincinnati Reds, who still displayed the effects of Larry Mac-Phail's team-building. In a repeat performance of 1939, Reds pitchers Bucky Walters and Paul Derringer both had 20-game years in 1940, Walters winning 22 and Derringer winning 20. Bill McKechnie's star first baseman, powerhouse Frank McCormick, led the league in hits for the third straight year, and was voted Most Valuable Player. The Reds' second straight pennant was marred only by the 3 August suicide of second-string catcher Willard Hershberger, who slashed his throat with a razor in the club's Boston hotel after several days of self-criticism for 'making a bad call.'

The Pirates' Debs Garms, who hit .355, was named league batting champion of 1940, even though he played in only 103 games (358 times at bat). The

Below: Larry MacPhail (left), the ex-Dodger boss who served as a lieutenant colonel in the US Army during World War II, gets the lowdown from his successor, Branch Rickey.

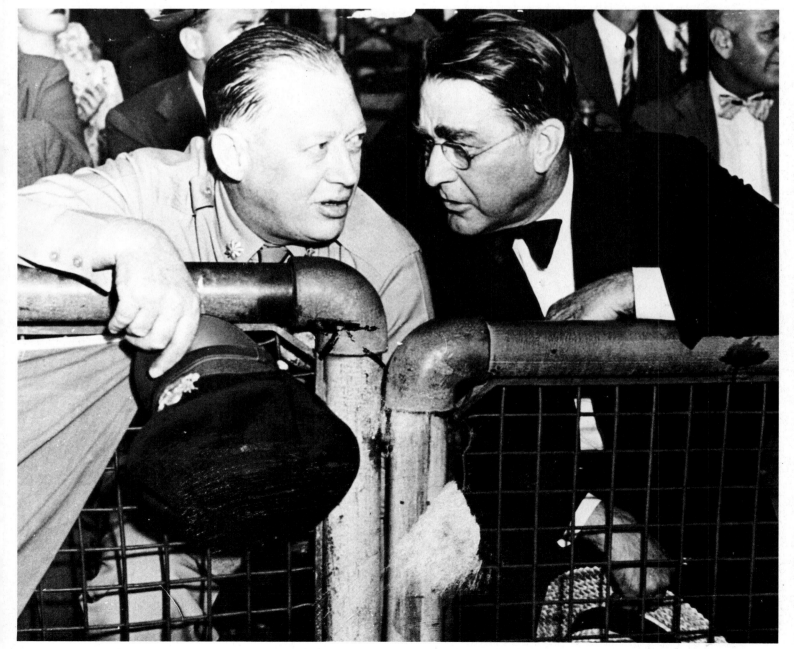

Above: Pete Reiser warms up. Harold Patrick 'Pistol Pete' Reiser played the outfield for the Dodgers (1940-42 and 1946-48), the Braves (1949-50), the Pirates (1951) and the Cleveland Indians (1952), and had a .295 batting average.

Top right: Pitcher John Whitlow 'Whit' Wyatt and manager Leo Durocher of the Dodgers protest umpire Bill McGowan's call.

Giants, the Cardinals and the Pirates introduced regular night games during the 1940 season, leaving only the Braves and the Cubs yet to join Larry Mac-Phail's arc-light revolution.

On 19 June, slugger Joe Medwick, who had been purchased by MacPhail for the Dodgers from St Louis one week earlier for $125,000, was traveling in an elevator in the Hotel New Yorker with Dodger manager Leo Durocher and former teammate Cardinal right-hander Bob Bowman. Medwick and Durocher took the opportunity to needle Bowman, who was scheduled to start against them in a game that afternoon. As they left the elevator, Bowman's parting words were, 'I'll take care of both of you this after-noon.'

On Medwick's first trip to bat, a fastball from Bow-man struck him in the head and rendered him uncon-scious. The Dodgers grabbed bats and charged the pitcher. As soon as Medwick was safely removed to the hospital, Larry MacPhail called National League President Ford Frick and demanded that Bowman be banned from baseball for life. Frick rejected Mac-Phail's request, the game went on with Bowman re-moved, and after about a week Medwick rejoined the Dodgers, but he was never to be the powerhouse hit-ter he had been for the Cardinals.

Larry MacPhail, who had created pennant winners from a moribund Cincinnati club in 1939 and 1940, signed on as general manager for Brooklyn in 1938, and immediately began rebuilding a Dodgers club which had not won a pennant since 1920. Spending lavishly, he installed lights in Ebbets Field, and in 1939 hired rambunctious Leo Durocher as manager. MacPhail and Durocher formed a powerful, volatile combination that made Brooklyn one of the most exciting and disliked clubs in the league. Battling each other as they battled for pennants, MacPhail fired and rehired Durocher at least once even before his first season as manager began.

Only somewhat daunted by the denting of prize acquisition Joe Medwick, MacPhail proceeded to plug up leaks in a Dodger squad that had come in second to Cincinnati in 1940 by purchasing hurler Kirby Higbe – who won 20 games in 1941 – from the Phillies, catcher Mickey Owen from the Cardinals and Billy Herman from Chicago. Other MacPhail acquisitions included first baseman Dolf Camilli and former American Leaguers pitcher Whitlow Wyatt and outfielder Dixie Walker, 'the Peepul's Cherce.' Wyatt won 22 games in 1941, including seven shutouts, for a 2.34 ERA, his best year ever.

Shortstop Pee Wee Reese and centerfielder Pete Reiser were also MacPhail finds. Reese, an excellent shortstop who played for the Dodgers for 16 years, was never a great hitter, but he was a fast, smart player who excelled at all the intangibles, and was usually found at the center of any Dodger rally. 'Pistol Pete' Reiser, a tremendously exciting player and one of the great centerfielders of the National League, hit .343 in his first full season to become, at 22, the youngest player to take the National League batting title. In 1941, Reiser led the league in hitting, slugging, runs, doubles and triples, and came in second, sandwiched between teammates Dolf Camilli and Whit Wyatt, in the balloting for Most Valued Player.

1941 saw a tight race between the Dodgers and the Cardinals all the way, with the lead changing 27 times during the season. The Cardinals led 11 times, the Dodgers seven, and the teams were tied nine times. Not until the 99th game did the Dodgers, who won 100 games for the first time in their history, clinch the pennant, and their 2½-game edge over the Cardinals might not have happened at all if a flood of injuries hadn't sidelined some of St Louis's best players. Experiencing some bad breaks of their own, the Dodgers dropped the World Series to the Yankees, 4-1.

In a game against Pittsburgh on 18 September, Leo Durocher's violent reaction to a call by umpire George Magerkurth caused him to be ejected from the game and fined $150. The next day, in Philadelphia, the Lip ran into Ted Meier of the Associated Press, who questioned him about the previous day's events. Durocher responded by knocking Meier down. Bystanders separated the two, and they parted after shaking hands.

On the occasion of the Dodger victory celebration, which was to be held at Grand Central Terminal, Durocher was again fired by general manager MacPhail. While the team was returning from New York to Boston, Durocher, fearing some of the players might slip off to avoid the celebration, prevented the train from stopping at 125th Street. Unknown to him, MacPhail had planned to board the train at 125th Street to join his team in its hour of glory. Outraged because the train hadn't stopped, when MacPhail arrived at Grand Central he greeted his manager with, 'You're fired!' but rehired him the next day when he heard the whole story.

Expecting an easy repeat of 1941, the Dodgers built up a 10-game lead by mid-August 1942. By this time every team in the league had become familiar with their beanballs, fists, spikes and mouthy manager. Among the few who felt that the pennant wasn't securely Brooklyn's yet was Larry MacPhail, who invaded the clubhouse one day to caution his team against the Cardinals and warn them that they ought to be 20 games up. MacPhail declined a bet against

Left: Stanley Frank 'Stan the Man' Musial was a star in the outfield and at first base for the Cardinals from 1941 to 1963 (with service time off in 1945). He had 3630 hits, 475 home runs and a batting average of .331. He was elected to the Hall of Fame in 1969.

Dixie Walker, who maintained that the Bums would finish no less than eight games ahead of St Louis.

Unfortunately for the Dodgers, MacPhail's misgivings proved to be correct. The Cardinals put on the greatest stretch run in history, winning 43 of their last 51 games – 34 of their last 40, including 21 of 26 in September – to take the flag from the Dodgers by two games, 106-104.

A heart-breaking injury suffered by Pete Reiser in July contributed to the Dodger defeat. The accident-prone Reiser, considered by many who saw him before this accident to be the greatest natural ball player of all time, was batting .390 when, with characteristic enthusiasm, he ran into an outfield wall chasing a ball in St Louis. Hospitalized with a severe concussion, he returned to the lineup too soon, as was then the practice, and his average dropped to .310 as he finished out the season playing through headaches, dizzy spells and double vision. Although there were flashes of the old Reiser after that – he stole home seven times in 1946 – 'Pistol Pete' was never quite the same.

Be that as it may, the Cardinals of 1942 were quite capable of standing on their own. Twenty-two of their 25-man roster came from the St Louis farm system. Many consider this team, which was to take four pennants in five years, one of the greatest National League teams of all time. Heading the strong pitching staff was Mort Cooper, winning 22 games and the Most Valuable Player Award for a 1.77 ERA and the best year of his career. He was supported by Johnny Beazley, with 21 wins in 1942, Ernie White, Howie Pollett and Max Lanier, all recording a team ERA of 2.55. Marty Marion played peerless shortstop, and Mort Cooper's brother Walker played behind the plate. Enos Slaughter and Terry Moore in the outfield were joined by a rookie named Stan Musial.

Stanislaus Musial had started in the minors as a pitcher, but a shoulder injury forced him to concentrate on hitting. Brought up to the Cardinals at the end of 1941, he hit .426 in 12 games, and in his first full season averaged .315. Modest, likeable, and one of the most popular players in National League history, beginning with his rookie year he batted well over .300 for 16 consecutive seasons, totally dominating league hitting for more than a decade. His popularity was such that it transcended the usual team loyalties – it was hypercritical Brooklyn fans admiring his style at Ebbets Field who first called him 'Stan the Man.'

The Man hit his stride in 1943, when as Most Valuable Player he led the league in hitting (.357), hits

Right: Rip Sewell demonstrates his 'eephus' pitch to catcher Al Lopez. Truett Banks 'Rip' Sewell was famous for this blooper pitch when he played for the Tigers (1932) and the Pirates (1938-49). He won 143 games in his 13-year career, and carried an earned run average of 3.48.
Below: Elmer Riddle pitched for the Reds (1939-47) and the Pirates (1948-49).

(220), doubles (48), triples (20), total bases (347) and slugging (.562); and came in second in runs with 108. His best season wasn't until 1948, but in 1962, in his 42nd year, he still managed to hit .330, just one point below his lifetime average. In the 22 years of his career, Stan Musial won seven batting titles and led the league six times in hits, eight times in doubles, five times in triples and six times in slugging. A strong defensive outfielder and an excellent base runner, Stan the Man remained accessible and considerate to fans and writers even as he rose to world fame, and was a truly loved ballplayer. When he retired, the city of St Louis honored him by commissioning a statue of the slugger and placing it outside the stadium.

Despite the Cardinals' great stretch drive of 1942, few people were prepared to believe that they had a chance against the Yankees, a club that had won its last eight World Series contests, and which in fact hadn't lost since the Cardinals beat them in 1926. In the first game, the Yankees were leading 7-0, but with two outs in the ninth inning, the Cardinals scored four

runs. They lost the game but, according to announcer Dizzy Dean, that was 'just the shot in the arm our boys needed.' The Cardinals swept the next four games of the Series, rounding out their incredible year of 1942 with a resounding defeat of the Yankees.

By the beginning of the 1942 season, American participation in the war was in full swing, and 161 National League players were already serving in the armed forces. After the end of the 1942 season, Larry MacPhail left the Dodgers to accept a commission as lieutenant colonel in the Service of Supply, and was replaced by Branch Rickey, who signed on for a five-year contract. Most of the superstars of the 1930s were off to war by the end of 1943. More than 1000 major leaguers – a 60 percent turnover of personnel – would don military uniforms by 1944.

Only a few good players remained. Stan Musial's children exempted him from the draft until 1945, when he entered the Navy, but by then the major leagues, filled with 4-F's, overage players, youngsters and a handful of Latin-Americans, were no longer playing major-league ball. In 1944, Cincinnati, with two infield positions held down by epileptics, sent fifteen-year-old Joe Nuxhall to the mound. The Waner brothers (Paul collected his 3000th hit in 1942), Debs Garms and Pepper Martin were among the elderly who returned to the diamond during what is often charitably referred to as the caretaking era.

Lack of talent was compounded by transportation restrictions – temporarily ending spring training in the South – low salaries in an inflated wartime economy, and shortages of equipment and food. Everyone knew that this was not really baseball, but the fans gave no sign of deserting the game. Although attendance slumped considerably in 1942-1943, it picked up rapidly in 1944-1945, topping all records since 1930 and giving hope for the postwar future. During the war every major-league team except the Yankees stepped up radio broadcasting, a factor

which probably increased interest in the game, and in 1944, American League attendance topped the 5 million mark for the first time since 1940. The World Series of 1945, which one sportswriter characterized as a test to see which wartime 'team' could lose first, set a new record for attendance and profit.

During the war years baseball was classified as a non-essential industry but, contrary to official treatment in World War I, the game was encouraged and even exhorted to continue as a morale builder and a diversion. Early in 1942, in response to a letter from Commissioner Landis, President Roosevelt wrote his famous 'green light' letter, lauding baseball for its contribution to sustaining national morale, and urging the game to 'Carry on to the fullest extent consistent with the primary purpose of winning the war.' In 1943, Manpower Commissioner Paul V McNutt even permitted ballplayers to leave essential winter factory jobs to play ball.

Among the many players who entered the service in 1943 were Pee Wee Reese and Pete Reiser of the Dodgers and John Beazley and Terry Moore of the

Above: A big league reunion is held by three former baseball players at a camp in the Pacific. Left is Marine PFC James 'Big Jim' Bivin, a former Phillies pitcher. Center is Army Lieutenant John Thomas 'Long Tom' Winsett, a former outfielder for the Red Sox, Cardinals and Dodgers. Right is Marine Corporal Calvin Leavell 'Preacher' Dorsett, a former pitcher with the Indians.
Top: While soldiers of two units are relaxing with a game of baseball in Luxembourg during World War II, a detonation charge is set off in the background – a reminder of the grim business of war.

Above: Outfielder Bill Nicholson in batting practice. In his 16 years with the Cubs and Phillies (1939-53), William Beck 'Swish' Nicholson hit 235 home runs, batted in 948 runs and had an average of .268.

Below: Left to right – Will Harridge, Judge Kenesaw Mountain Landis and Ford Frick – the professional baseball hierarchy.

Cardinals. Even though the Cards lost many of their regulars, because of their extensive farm system they were able to come up with more competent replacements than any other National League team. Mort Cooper was still on hand, and Stan Musial didn't enter the Navy until 1945. It was small wonder that St Louis swept to easy victories in 1943 and 1944, taking three flags in a row.

Musial batted .357 to lead the league in his 1943 MVP year, and hit a respectable .347 in 1944. The Yankees took their revenge on the Cardinals for 1942 by taking the 1943 World Series in five games, but the Cards came back to take the Series from the Browns in six games in 1944, in the first World Series played entirely west of the Mississippi. Redbird second baseman Emil Verban batted .421 for the Series, reportedly out of

anger at the Browns for seating his wife behind a post for three of the games.

Chalking up his third 20-game season in a row, Mort Cooper won 22 games for the Cardinals in 1944. Ted Wilks, released by the Army because of a stomach ulcer, was 17-4, and George Munger won 11 of 14 games before his induction in July. The Most Valuable Player Award stayed in St Louis for the second straight year, going to 'Mr Shortstop' Marty Marion. In the outstanding pitching achievement of the year, Boston righthander Jim Tobin pitched two no-hitters, blanking the Dodgers, 2-0 on 27 April, and the Phillies, 7-0 on 22 June.

Baseball's first Commissioner, Kenesaw Mountain Landis, died on 25 November 1944, five days after his 78th birthday, after 44 years of service. On 24 April 1945, club owners of both leagues elected gung-ho 'Ah love baseball' Albert Benjamin 'Happy' Chandler to replace him. The former governor and United States Senator from Kentucky was signed to a seven-year contract at $50,000 a year.

In 1945, the Cubs, spearheaded by first baseman Phil Cavarretta, finished three games ahead of second-place St Louis to take the last pennant they would win for decades. Stan Musial's absence in the Navy helped, but Cavarretta turned in a respectable .355 average to take the MVP Award and the league batting championship, and righthander Hank Borowy, acquired by the Cubs at the end of July from the Yankees, was 11-2 for the Bruins, becoming the only pitcher ever to win 20 games while dividing a season between two leagues.

The real batting achievement of the 1945 season went to Boston outfielder Tommy Holmes, who established a new National League record for hitting safely in 37 consecutive games. During his streak, which lasted from 6 June through 8 July, he batted .423, although his season average of .352 fell three points short of league-leading MVP Cavarretta.

The war was over. Even before the end of the pennant race, some regular players managed to slip out of the military and back into baseball uniform. Perhaps it was public jubilation at the successful conclusion of the wars in Europe and the Pacific that brought record numbers of fans to the World Series – the Cubs lost to the Tigers in seven – or perhaps it was anticipation of the return to the big-name heroes that drew the public to the parks. Baseball had more than weathered the war, and with profits and attendance finally rising above Depression and wartime lows, everyone looked forward to the coming season.

Having waited patiently for the right moment, Branch Rickey chose this happy time of rising expectations and social upheaval to break baseball's color line by signing three black players for the Dodgers. Pitchers Ray Partlow and John Wright, of the Newark Eagles, went to Three Rivers, Quebec. Shortstop Jackie Robinson, who had played with the Kansas City Monarchs, was signed on 28 August 1945 and sent to the Dodger's top farm club in Montreal, in the International League. Jackie Robinson, one of the most exciting players of his era, was destined to be the first black to play major-league ball in the 20th century.

Excluded from National League baseball in the 1880s by an unwritten but ironclad 'gentlemen's agreement,' blacks had formed their own leagues, and could boast players the equal of any in the majors. Exhibition games between blacks and white major leaguers left no doubt about the quality of black talent. Dizzy Dean once remarked, 'I have played against a Negro All-Star team that was so good, we

didn't think we had an even chance against them.' But despite antidiscrimination laws, baseball remained steadfastly segregated.

In 1943, when Bill Veeck, Jr proposed to purchase the limping Phillies and build the club up with black players, including the legendary pitcher Satchel Paige, he was warned off by Commissioner Landis and League President Ford Frick, and the club was sold elsewhere for less than he had offered. At about the same time, under similar pressure, Pittsburgh Pirate President William Benswanger called off tryouts for Roy Campanella, Sam Hughes and Dave Barnhill. In 1901, when John J McGraw, then managing the Orioles, tried to sneak black second baseman Charlie Grant onto his team by passing him off as a full-blooded Cherokee, Chicago White Sox President Charlie Comiskey – who had seen Grant play with the Chicago Columbia Eagles in the black leagues – made sure it didn't happen. When Jackie Robinson arrived in Montreal 44 years later, the manager of the Dodger farm team asked Branch Rickey, 'Do you really think a nigger's a human being?'

Rickey's motives in choosing Jackie Robinson as a test case for the 1947 season were mixed, and will probably remain forever obscure. Certainly Robinson, a college graduate and a superior infielder, was

the right man, capable of enduring the ordeal he was about to go through. But whatever Rickey's moral imperative, no one doubts that he was driven at least as strongly by his legendary fondness of the dollar. Black players represented a vast, untapped reservoir of major-league talent, and Rickey was convinced that the Dodgers would get an edge on other teams if they were the first to sign blacks. He was evidently correct, as the Dodgers became the dominant team in the league for a decade following Robinson's debut, and the National League gained a supremacy over the American League that still holds today. The Yankees didn't play a black until eight years after the Dodgers, the White Sox not until 12 years later.

When Jackie Robinson came up to the Dodgers in 1947 he faced years of vicious insults at every level. The Dodgers themselves talked of circulating a petition asking that Robinson not be brought up. Dixie Walker asked to be and was traded. The Phillies, and manager Ben Chapman in particular, were warned by Ford Frick to curb their abuse. The Dodgers were for a time obliged to move spring training out of the American South to Cuba.

Fortunately, Robinson proved to be a superstar ballplayer and a man with enough restraint to integrate the league. Other blacks followed after he broke

Jack Roosevelt Robinson at the plate. Jackie was the courageous player who broke the color barrier in baseball, playing both the infield and the outfield in his ten-year career with the Brooklyn Dodgers (1947-56). He was voted Rookie of the Year in 1947, Most Valuable Player in 1949, elected to the Hall of Fame in 1962 and had a lifetime .311 batting average.

Sal Maglie warms up. Salvatore Anthony 'The Barber' Maglie pitched for ten years in the majors, with time off for the Mexican League. He started with the Giants (1945, 1950-55), went to the Cleveland Indians (1955-56), then to the Dodgers (1956-57), then to the Yankees (1957-58) and finally to the Cardinals (1958). He had a phenomenal 119-62 record with a 3.15 ERA.

Far right: Baseball Commissioner A B 'Happy' Chandler (former governor of Kentucky) throws out the first ball at the World Series in 1947.

Hausman and Danny Gardella. The Cardinals lost their star pitcher, Max Lanier, as well as pitcher Fred Martin and infielder Lou Klein. The Dodgers lost outfielder Luis Olmo and their regular catcher, Mickey Owen. Just back from a year in the Navy, Stan Musial considered a $65,000 advance against a five-year offer of $130,000, but opted to remain with the Cardinals.

American owners, with the blessings of Commissioner Chandler, outlawed the Mexican League and blacklisted any jumping players, vowing they would be barred from organized baseball for five years if they ever returned. As it turned out, the Mexican League proved to be a makeshift affair, and most of the jumpers were quickly disenchanted. Mickey Owen, the first of the returnees, came back to the States in August. But both American players and the Mexican Government were infuriated by the black-listing and the declaration of illegality.

When Danny Gardella, who jumped to the Mexican League from the Giants, took the matter of his black-listing to the courts, baseball executives, who knew their legal position was weak, rescinded the blacklists and issued amnesties to all fugitive players. No players were ever barred from returning to the American majors for much more than three years. Gardella was also paid an out-of-court settlement to drop his suit in 1949. Baseball men were beginning to understand that their regulations – such as the 'gentlemen's agreement' barring blacks – were subject to some limitations, and even to federal court jurisdiction if they involved international matters or matters of personal rights.

the ice, until by the 1960s more than 100 black players had joined the majors. In 1967, 23 blacks in the National League and 17 blacks in the American League accounted for well over half of the base hits made that year. A recent study has shown that black pitchers have consistently better averages than white pitchers, and black batters generally hit harder and have higher averages than do whites, but the most profitable endorsements and peripheral rewards still go primarily to whites.

In 1946, with the nation just beginning to adjust to a peacetime economy, National League club owners faced two separate but related precedent-setting challenges. In the spring, Mexican millionaire Jorge Pascual and his four brothers, attempting to create a Mexican League to compete with the American majors, began luring away top American players by offering them princely salaries. Pascual succeeded in enticing away some excellent players, many of whom were dissatisfied with the domestic pay scale. The Giants lost seven players to the Mexican League: pitchers Sal Maglie and relief star Ace Adams, Harry Feldman, Adrian Zabala, Roy Zimmerman, George

In the spring of 1946, at the same time that major strikes were taking place throughout the United States, onetime examiner for the National Labor Relations Board, Harvard lawyer Robert Murphy, formed the American Baseball Guild to represent players against owners. On 7 June, under Murphy's direction, the Pirates came very close to striking against Pittsburgh owner Bill Benswanger. Players across the league were remarkably united in their grievances, and the owners realized that they were not in a strong position, especially with the Mexican League checkbook ready to snap up players who were tired of waiting for things to get better.

Commissioner Chandler, hoping to outflank the formation of a serious players' union, invited the players, who were dissatisfied with their lack of financial security, to send delegates to discuss their grievances. In September the owners granted a number of concessions to the players, really a sort of players 'magna charta,' which included a $5000 minimum salary, limit of salary cuts to 25 percent per year, a pension fund bolstered by club payments, shorter spring training, free medical benefits and an allowance for spring training – $25 per week – known ever since as 'Murphy Money.' Player organization was stopped short of full unionization, but the incident led in time to the formation of the powerful Major League Baseball Players' Association.

In 1946, as if picking up where they left off, the Dodgers and the Cardinals ran a tight and exciting pennant race. At the end of the season the clubs were tied 96-58, necessitating the first pennant play-off in major-league history. The Cardinals took the first two

of the best two-out-of-three series and went on to even greater glory by defeating the heavily-favored Red Sox in the World Series, 4-3. Leo Durocher, managing the Dodgers, enunciated the famous 'Nice guys finish last' in the dugout before a game at the Polo Grounds on 5 July. He was referring to famous nice guy 'McGraw's Little Boy' Mel Ott, who was managing the Giants.

Stan Musial helped his team to the pennant with a league-leading .365 average, and also led the league in doubles, triples, hits, runs, slugging and total bases. Pittsburgh's Ralph Kiner led the league in homers, with 23. The 23-year-old rookie outfielder, hitting high and far, would continue to tie or lead the league in home runs for his first seven seasons. Also in 1946, the Braves became the seventh National League team to install arc-lights, leaving the Cubs as the last hold-outs (as they remain to this day).

During the spring training exhibition season of 1947 in Havana, Leo Durocher climaxed a series of run-ins with baseball's top executives when he heckled his former boss Larry MacPhail, now with the Yankees, who was apparently entertaining two well-known gamblers in a private box behind the Yankee dugout. Quipped Durocher, who had been accused of gambling on more than one occasion, 'Are there two sets of rules, one for managers, and one for owners?'

MacPhail, who was already involved in an acrimonious dispute with Dodger general manager Branch Rickey which featured public name-calling, did not take kindly to Durocher's remarks. Durocher further entered the fray by telling the *Brooklyn Eagle*

Far left: Ralph McPherran Kiner, who hit 369 in his 10 years in the majors, with the Pirates (1946-53), the Cubs (1953-54) and the Indians (1954). This outfielder led the league seven times in home run production and had a .256 average; he also batted .429 in the only World Series he appeared in. A Hall of Famer, he is now an announcer for the New York Mets.

Below: Bert Shotten (left) greets Mel Ott. Burton Edwin 'Barney' Shotten had had a so-so career as a player, playing the outfield for the Browns, the Senators and the Cardinals from 1909 to 1923, but he came into his own as a manager with Philadelphia (1928-33), Cincinnati (1934) and Brooklyn (1947-50). In his four years at Brooklyn, he won two pennants and one World Series. Ott was the manager of the Giants in 1947 and 1948.

that MacPhail had offered him the management of the Yankees. McPhail retorted that the reverse was true, that Durocher had solicited the job from him, and filed a bill of particulars with Commissioner Chandler accusing Durocher of 'conduct detrimental to base-ball.'

After a couple of hearings, Commissioner Chandler, who seemed to harbor a particular dislike for Durocher, suspended the Lip from baseball for one year. The Yankees and the Dodgers were both fined $2000 each for dragging baseball's good name though the mud, and old-timer Burt Shotton was called out of semi-retirement to replace Durocher for the year.

At the very height of the commotion – Durocher was suspended about one week before the opening of the season – the Dodgers announced that they had purchased Jackie Robinson's contract from Montreal. Major-league baseball was now officially integrated.

Robinson's rookie season was greeted with a flood of racial incidents, ranging from abuse by some of his teammates to serious tension in many cities. The Cardinals threatened to strike rather than appear on the same field with a black man. League President Ford Frick responded immediately and forcefully, vowing to suspend any player who struck. 'I do not care if half the league strikes. Those who do it will encounter quick retribution. All will be suspended and I do not care if it wrecks the National League for five years. This is the United States of America and one citizen has as much right to play as another.'

There was no strike. Robinson, despite a hellish reception, managed to play better than competent ball, batting .297 and stealing 29 bases. Named Rookie of the Year, his performance undoubtedly helped his team take the pennant, and he became the mainstay of a Dodgers club that was to win six pennants in the next ten years.

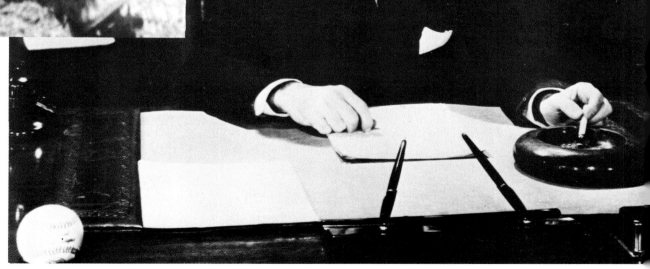

Above: Ewell 'The Whip' Blackwell, described as a 'buggy whip with ears,' winds up. Blackwell pitched for the Reds (1942-52), the Yankees (1952-53) and Kansas City (1955). His best year was 1947, when he won 22 and lost eight.
Right: Ford Frick, the president of the National League.

Pitching for fifth-place Cincinnati, righthander Ewell Blackwell had a 22-8 season that included 16 wins in a row, and came close to duplicating teammate Johnny Vander Meer's double no-hitters. After no-hitting the Braves on 18 June, Blackwell had only two outs to go to win a second consecutive no-hitter when Eddie Stanky of the Dodgers grounded a single through his legs. Curiously, the Dodgers and the Braves were the same two clubs Vander Meer won his back-to-back no-hitters from. Asked what he was thinking while he watched his teammate from the dugout, Vander Meer replied that if Blackwell did it, 'I wanted to be the first one out there to shake his hand.'

In his second year, Ralph Kiner hit 51 home runs for his last-place Pittsburgh team to tie Johnny Mize of the Giants for the 1947 league title. Mize and Kiner became the second and third players in National League history, after Hack Wilson, to hit more than 50 home runs in one year. The fourth-place Giants, with big guns Mize hitting 51 homers, Willard Marshal 36, Walker Cooper 35 and Bobby Thomson 29, set a new team home run record with 221.

Postwar baseball had entered a lucrative period. The National League became the first league to pass the 10 million attendance mark, with 10,388,470 paying spectators attending National League games in 1947.

Leo Durocher returned to the Dodgers in 1948, but only for half a season. Giant owner Horace Stoneham, who was tired of likeable but ineffectual manager Mel Ott, and Branch Rickey, who had apparently had enough of lippy Leo and his squabbles with his players, arranged one of the most shocking managerial shifts in baseball history. Stoneham, who went to Rickey to ask for his approval to approach Burt Shot-

ton to replace Ott, found himself being offered Durocher instead. He accepted the offer, Leo agreed, and the Lip took up his new duties on 16 July. Branch Rickey called Burt Shotton back to manage the Dodgers, and Mel Ott accepted a position in the Giant front office as assistant to farm director Carl Hubbell.

For the first time in 34 years, the Boston Braves, an unremarkable team except for their pitchers, won a pennant, finishing 6½ games in front of the Cardinals. Righthander Johnny Sain won 24 games and lefthander Warren Spahn won 15, the duo's exploits inspiring the doggerel verse, 'Spahn and Sain/Then pray for rain.' They each won a game in the World Series, but the Braves lost to the Indians, 6-2.

Stan Musial won another Most Valuable Player Award in 1948, in what was his best year and the finest all-round year of any National League hitter since the war. The Man led the league in eight offensive categories, and came just one run short of tying for the league home run lead of 40, which was again shared by Ralph Kiner and Johnny Mize.

In his third year in the league, Jackie Robinson, now at second base, was voted the National League's Most Valuable Player by a wide margin. Robinson, in his best year ever, led the league with a .342 batting average, scored 122 runs and drove in 124. His league-leading 37 stolen bases was a sum greater than the team totals of the Cardinals, Phillies, Braves and Reds.

Leo Durocher, backed up by Giant coaches Fred Fitzsimmons and Frank Frisch, was exonerated at a hearing before Commissioner Chandler of the charge of slugging a fan on 28 April after a game at the Polo Grounds. As a result of the episode, however, Giant owner Horace Stoneham instituted a policy of keeping all spectators off the playing field until all personnel of both teams reached their clubhouses.

National League players who had been barred for jumping to the Mexican League were permitted to return to play this year (Max Lanier and Fred Martin dropped a $2,500,000 damage suit and Danny Gardella withdrew his $500,000 suit), and Mrs Ernie Bonham received the first death benefits of the player pension fund. Hurler Ernie Bonham died on 15 September following abdominal surgery. His widow received $90 a month for ten years.

Fired by Jackie Robinson's stellar year, the Dodgers took the 1949 pennant. In what was to become the tension-filled trademark style of this club, they clinched the flag in the tenth inning of the last game of the season, edging out the Cardinals by one game.

With other clubs still reluctant to sign blacks, the Dodgers had their pick of the finest black talent, and made choices that helped keep them on top for years. 1949 saw Roy Campanella and Don Newcombe play their first full seasons with the Dodgers. Largely because of Robinson's success, the Giants signed their first two blacks in 1949, Hank Thompson, who had played with the St Louis Browns in 1947, and Monte Irvin, from the Newark Eagles. Both first went to the Giants' Jersey City team.

The Dodgers almost signed Larry Doby, but Branch Rickey, learning that Bill Veeck wanted to sign him for Cleveland to integrate the American League, let the young power-hitter go, to further 'the cause,' as he put it. The pennant-winning 1949 Dodger club dropped the Series to the Yankees (their 12th Series win), but this team, put together by Branch Rickey, which in addition to its great black players included Pee Wee Reese, Gil Hodges, Billy Cox, Carl Furillo and Duke Snider, went on to dominate the 1950s as few clubs have ever dominated any decade.

Far left: Hall of Famer Warren Edward Spahn pitched for the Braves from 1942 to 1964 – first in Boston and then in Milwaukee – before spending 1965 with the Giants. He won 363 games and had an ERA of 3.09.

CHAPTER FIVE

Dodger Dynasty

Home run hitters drive Cadillacs, singles hitters drive Fords.

Ralph Kiner

The team Branch Rickey built in Brooklyn after he took over from Larry MacPhail in 1942 was not only the greatest of his incredible career, but arguably the greatest National League team of all time. In the ten-year period 1947-1956, the Dodgers won six pennants and came in tight second three times. Only in 1948 when they came in third, 7½ games behind Boston, were they really out of the race. If the Dodgers had ended the seasons of 1946, 1950 and 1951 with winning rather than losing games, they would have won nine pennants in 11 years, including five in a row. If they had won 19 more games in the 11-year stretch 1946-1956, they could have won 11 pennants in 11 years.

The Dodger lineup that formed the guts of the 1949 pennant-winners remained essentially intact for the next decade, with Reese the only holdover from MacPhail's 1941 champions. He and Campanella, Snider, Hodges and Furillo remained in the lineup and at their positions until the Dodger move to Los Angeles in 1958. Third baseman Billy Cox left the Dodgers in 1954, and after Jim 'Junior' Gilliam arrived to take over

second base in 1953, Jackie Robinson alternated between third base and the outfield for his remaining four years with the club.

The trio of Snider, Hodges and Campanella had five seasons in which they hit over 100 homers combined, and Robinson and Reese were the league's best base stealers. Defensively, Furillo, Cox, Snider, Reese, Robinson, Hodges and Campanella were all at one time or another considered the best in the league at their positions. The only weakness in the club – and probably the reason they didn't win every pennant of their era – was lack of depth in their pitching staff. The only pitchers with any sustained success were Don Newcombe, who won 20 games three times and 17 or more five times, and Carl Erskine, who won at least 11 games for six straight seasons. Preacher Roe and Clem Labine had brief flashes of excellence, but otherwise, in marked contrast to the stability of the team as a whole, inconsistent hurlers, some with moments of great brilliance, came and went.

At the beginning of the 1950s, the club was young, and it could hit and run and throw. As the century reached its mid-point and the National League

Below: Carl Anthony Furillo, also known as 'Skoonj' or 'The Reading Rifle,' played the outfield for the Dodgers (1946-60). Hitting .299, he batted in 1058 runs.

entered the last quarter of its first 100 years, the team that Rickey built showed its stuff by taking five of the 1950s pennants, coming in second three times and finishing out of the first division only once in the decade.

The 1950 pennant went to the Phillies. Nicknamed the 'Whiz Kids' for their spirited play and their youth – their average age was only 26 – the first Phillies pennant in 35 years climaxed seven years of rebuilding by owner Robert Carpenter, a heavy investor in the postwar bonus boom that saw half a dozen young players collect over $50,000 each. The Phillies' first flag win since 1915 was spearheaded by a pitching staff which featured Robin Roberts, their first 20-game winner since 1917; Curt Simmons, who won 17 games before being inducted into the Army; and relief ace Jim Konstanty, whose 16 wins in 74 relief appearances earned him the Most Valuable Player Award, the first time the award ever went to a relief pitcher.

With 11 games remaining in the season, the Phillies were seven games up, but injuries to two starting pitchers and Curt Simmons's September induction precipitated a decline which cost the club eight of their next ten games. As fate would have it, the Phillies, only one game ahead, faced the Dodgers at Ebbets Field on 1 October.

Manager Eddie Sawyer chose Robin Roberts to save the pennant from Brooklyn's Don Newcombe. For Roberts, now in his third National League season, this was the third start in five days. He held Newcombe to a 1-1 standoff until the bottom of the ninth inning, when the Dodgers put men on first and second with none out. Duke Snider singled to center, and center fielder Richie Ashburn, who with the rest of the Phillies had been expecting a bunt, managed to scoop up the ball and throw Cal Abrams out at the plate.

Carl Furillo fouled out and Gil Hodges was retired on a fly ball. In the top of the tenth inning, Dick Sisler, son of first base immortal George Sisler, hit a three-run homer to save the day. His father, now the Dodgers' chief scout, was there to see his son help Robin Roberts to the first of six consecutive 20-games seasons.

On 31 August, Dodger first baseman Gil Hodges hit four home runs in the course of a 19-3 victory over the Braves at Ebbets Field to become the fourth National Leaguer, the sixth major-leaguer, and the first National Leaguer in the 20th century to hit four homers in a game. On 13 September, Giant pitcher Sal Maglie was only four outs away from breaking Carl

Opposite: Carl Daniel Erskine, pitcher for the Dodgers (1948-59).
Opposite inset: Hall of Famer Robert Evan Roberts pitched from 1948 to 1966, winning 286 games.
Below right: Outfielder Don Richie 'Whitey' Ashburn played for the Phillies, Cubs and Giants from 1948 to 1962.
Below left: Donald 'Newk' Newcombe pitched for the Dodgers, Reds and Cleveland.

Hubbell's record of 46 and 1/3 consecutive scoreless innings when Pittsburgh's Gus Bell shattered his streak with a home run over the Polo Grounds' right field wall. Other 1950 business as usual included a 21-game year for Warren Spahn, another batting title for Stan Musial, and another home run title for Ralph Kiner.

In 1950 Grover Cleveland Alexander, who in 1915 pitched the Phillies to their only other pennant, died in St Paul, Nebraska in a room he rented out of his $150-a-month pension. Branch Rickey sold his interest in the Dodgers to Walter O'Malley and became general manager of the Pirates, Ford Frick was awarded another four years as National League president and major-league club owners, reflecting a growing distaste for the dictatorial style originated by Commissioner Landis, voted not to extend Commissioner Chandler's contract.

On 27 February 1951, the National League observed its 75th anniversary with a magnificent celebration at the Broadway Central Hotel, formerly known as the Grand Central Hotel, the place of the league's birth. A telegram from President Truman was read in which the chief executive called baseball 'our national sport' and made the following observation:

> The founders of the National League and the fans of that era never dreamed the game would achieve such popularity or there would be such inventions as radio and television to carry it to millions of Americans all over the world.

As the 1951 season began, what looked like an easy walk to the pennant for the Dodgers turned into a race that ended in one of the National League's most dramatic playoffs. The Dodgers took the lead on 13 May, while the Giants lost 11 of their first 12 games, and by mid-August, with a comfortable 13½ game lead on the second-place Giants, the Dodgers were

apparently invulnerable. But then something happened.

Leo Durocher, who took over the Giants in 1948, had been rebuilding a team he had inherited which featured a lot of power but not much running speed. Big Guns Mize, Cooper, Marshall and Sid Gordon were gone by 1951, and a crucial trade with the Braves had brought the Giants Alvin Dark and Eddy Stanky. Durocher was able to begin 1951 with Monte Irvin on first, Stanky at second, Dark at shortstop and Henry Thompson or Bobby Thomson at third. Bobby Thomson, Whitey Lockman and Don Mueller covered the outfield, with Lockman and Irvin switching places early in the season. Sal Maglie, who returned from the Mexican League in 1950 to win 18 games, headed a strong pitching staff which included Larry Jansen, Jim Hearn, lefty Dave Koslo and sinkerball doctor George Spencer.

Late in May, Durocher brought up a 20-year-old center fielder from the Giants' Minneapolis farm club named Willie Mays. In Leo's own words, Mays 'could do the five things you have to do to be a superstar: hit, hit with power, run, throw and field. And he had that other magic ingredient that turns a superstar into a super superstar. He lit up the room when he came in. He was a joy to be around.'

Not everyone would agree that Mays was a joy to be around, particularly sportswriters and the fans he often treated with disdain, but no one has ever questioned that the Giants' center fielder was one of the most spectacular players of all time, and ranks with Honus Wagner among the very best players in National League history. From his first season as Rookie of the Year, with a modest .274 average and 20 home runs, Willie Mays demonstrated that he was born to hit home runs, make incredible catches, incredible throws and run out from under his hat with incredible flashes of speed and a sensational style that inspired the Giants to overcome insurmountable odds to take the pennant.

Mays was to compile a record ranking him in the National League all-time top five in hits, home runs, runs, RBI's, slugging and extra base hits, but by those who saw him he will probably best be remembered for a fielding style and a base-running flair that made impossible plays look easy and easy plays look exciting. In one four-year stretch he stole 136 bases, leading the league each year. In six seasons he stole at least 20 bases and hit at least 20 home runs, and in two others he stole at least 30 bases and hit at least 30 home runs, a feat equalled by only one other player in National League history, Bobby Banks, who played with Mays in San Francisco and learned from him.

A player who could do everything, offensively as well as defensively, Mays had six seasons in which he hit more than 40 home runs and two in which he hit more than 50 home runs, and he could also hit for average, leading the league with .345 in 1954 and reaching his personal peak of .347 in 1958. Just how important he was to the Giants' success was demonstrated dramatically when he disappeared into the service after the beginning of the 1952 season.

It was only after Mays' appearance in 1951 that Durocher's Giants began to make the most historic dash toward a pennant since the run of the Miracle Boston Braves in 1914. Starting on 12 August, the Giants won 16 consecutive games until, by 9 September (with the Dodgers losing 9 out of 18), they were only 5½ games behind. Then the Giants won 16 of their last 20 (while the Dodgers lost 11) to force the pennant race into a playoff.

Jim Hearn took the opening game for the Giants, 3-1, and Clem Labine took the second for the Dodgers, 10-0. The Dodgers were leading in the deciding game 4-1 when, in the bottom of the ninth, the Giants launched a rally. Alvin Dark singled, Don Mueller singled and Monte Irvin pop-fouled out. Then Whitey Lockman doubled, driving Dark home and putting the tying runs on second and third. Brooklyn's Don Newcombe was replaced by righthander Ralph Branca, who faced Giant Bobby Thomson.

So far in the game Thomson had distinguished himself by getting caught in a rundown after heading to second without realizing that Lockman was already there. Thomson let Branca's first strike go by, but sent the second one into the left field stands to clear the bases and give the Giants the pennant with 'the home run heard round the world,' etching into baseball legend one of the most dramatic climaxes in National League history.

It is interesting to note that an estimated three million family television sets were turned to the dramatic playoffs between the Dodgers and the Giants, and a few million others viewed it from bars and lounges. By 1951, television was an important force in American sports, and the income to baseball from telecasts was soon to be a major factor in the first National League franchise shifts in over 50 years. Profits to baseball from telecasts had risen steadily since television was introduced in the late 1940s, and amounted to $27.5 million in 1966.

On 20 September, Ford Frick was elected to succeed Happy Chandler as baseball commissioner, and one week later Warren Giles, general manager of the Reds, was elected president of the National League, to succeed Frick.

The Dodgers came back strong to take pennants in 1952 and 1953. The Giants actually took the lead early in 1952, but after Willie Mays was inducted into the Army on 29 May, they lost eight of their next ten games, and never recovered. Don Newcombe of the Dodgers was also inducted, a loss somewhat mitigated by the arrival of rookie righthander relief pitcher Joe Black, whose 15-4 season included 15 saves. Brooklyn unveiled its own rookie, Hoyt Wilhelm, who continued to throw his impossible knuckle ball for 21 years through 1070 games in the majors, retiring in 1972 at the age of 49.

On the way to the 1952 pennant, the Dodgers set a modern major-league record when they scored 15 runs in the first inning of a game against the Reds. Twenty-one Dodgers went to the plate in that inning, with 19 in a row reaching base safely. On 19 June, Carl Erskine held the Cubs hitless for a 5-0 win. By walking opposing pitcher Willard Ramsdell in the third inning, Erskine just missed becoming the first pitcher in 30 years to pitch a perfect game during the regular season.

The Dodgers faced the Yankees in the World Series, taking the first, third and fifth games, but losing their sixth consecutive Series clash. Notable in failure was Gil Hodges, with 32 homers and 102 RBI's for the season, who went hitless in 21 Series at-bats. In his first season as league president, Warren Giles set something of a record by fining Leo Durocher three times, all for clashes with umpires.

1953 marked the first National League franchise shift in 53 years. Only five years before, the Boston Braves had attracted 1,455,439 fans in a pennant winning season, but with total attendance for 1952 at only 281,000 and losses of $600,000, on 18 March 1953 owner Lou Perini announced the transfer of the

Boston Braves to Milwaukee, citing sagging attendance and apathy on the part of the fans.

The move to Milwaukee paid off magnificently. The first 13 home games at Milwaukee showed an attendance total of 302,667, more than for all of 1952, and the Braves' 1,826,397 season attendance total marked a new National League record. 2,131,388 people paid to watch the Braves in 1954, and by 1957, with the Braves taking the first of two back-to-back pennants, attendance at Milwaukee topped 2 million for the fourth straight season, setting a new league record of 2,215,404. The thinking of club owners whose teams were struggling at the gate began to undergo some changes.

The Braves responded to their enthusiastic reception in Milwaukee in 1953 by moving from seventh to second place. Warren Spahn threw 23-7 for a 2.10 ERA year, the lowest of a career in which he 13 times won 20 or more games, while 21-year-old third baseman Eddie Mathews hit 47 homers to lead the league and end the seven-year reign of Ralph Kiner, who moved to the Cubs on 4 June. Kiner was also bested by Cincinnati's Ted Kluszewski and Brooklyn's Duke Snider and Roy Campanella, who took his second MVP.

From 13 May, the Braves were first or second in the pennant race. On 25 May, Braves righthander Max Surkant established a modern record by striking out eight consecutive batters. Lew Burdette won 15 games in the first of ten consecutive seasons in which he would win at least 10 games, Bill Bruton won the first of three consecutive stolen base titles and Joe Adcock hit 18 home runs.

Above: Edwin Lee 'Eddie' Mathews played third base for the Braves in Boston and Milwaukee (1952-65) and then went with them to Atlanta (1966). He went to Houston in 1967 and then switched to the American League and played for the Tigers (1967-68), hitting 512 home runs with a .271 batting average.

Only a Brooklyn club considered among the most powerful if not the most powerful in the history of the franchise was able to stop the rejuvenated Braves, but after taking the pennant by a whopping 13 games, the Bums once again lost to the Yankees in the World Series. Carl Erskine distinguished himself by striking out 14 Yankees in the third game, setting a new record, and Gil Hodges redeemed himself for his 1952 world championship performance by hitting .364 for the Series.

Charlie Dressen, who had managed the Dodgers to their last two pennants, found himself out of a job less than a week after the Series. When he formulated his demand for a three-year contract in terms of an ultimatum, the Dodgers, who preferred one-year contracts for managers, let him go, and owner O'Malley brought up Walter Alston from the Montreal (International League) farm club. Alston was unable to bring home the pennant in 1954, but he eventually helped the Dodgers to nine pennants, and signed 23 one-year contracts, ending his career with the Dodgers in Los Angeles.

Willie Mays came out of the Army stronger than when he went in, and it was a Giant team reinvigorated by his return that came out on top in 1954. Mays's batting average of .345 led the league, and he hit 41 home runs and 110 RBI's, with the usual spectacular fielding, for a 1954 Most Valuable Player Award performance that propelled his club to a finish five games ahead of the second-place Dodgers.

Johnny Antonelli, whom the Giants had acquired from the Braves in a trade for 1951 pennant hero Bobby Thomson, turned in a 21-7 season with a league-leading ERA for his new team. Don Mueller's average was second only to teammate Willie Mays'. In other hitting events of 1954, Stan Musial established a new major-league record when he hit five home runs in a doubleheader against the Giants on 2 May in St Louis, and Milwaukee's Joe Adcock hit four homers in one game against Brooklyn to equal the modern record. On 23 April, Milwaukee rookie Henry Aaron hit his first home run. Little attention was given to the homer he hit off Cardinal Vic Raschi, but it was the first of an amazing career which saw Aaron gain the all-time home run championship.

The Cleveland Indians, who set a new American League record with 111 wins, were highly favored to take the Series from the Giants, many thought in four games. But it was the Giants who swept the Series from the Indians, led by an incredible performance by James Lamar 'Dusty' Rhodes, whom Durocher had tried to trade at the beginning of the season, calling him the worst fielder he had ever seen.

Willie Mays lit up the first game with a spectacular catch that many regard as the most famous in World Series history. In the eighth inning, with the score tied at 2-2, two men on and none out, Mays caught Vic Wertz's 440-foot drive over his shoulder and returned it to the infield so fast that neither base runner could advance. In the tenth inning, with two Giants on, Dusty Rhodes was called in to pinch hit and produced a home run to win the game.

Rhodes hit a single driving in Mays in the fifth inning of the second game, and another homer driving in another run in the seventh inning. In the third game, a Rhodes single in the third inning drove in two runs. In his first four Series at-bats, Series MVP Rhodes got four hits – including two homers – and knocked in a total of seven runs.

This was the first National League Series win since 1946, and the first National League Series sweep since the Miracle Braves of 1914. The initial tendency to think of it as a fluke due to Rhodes's performance gave way over the passing years to the realization that the National League had now become baseball's power center. With the American League still proceeding cautiously in the signing of black players, most outstanding young black players chose to sign on with National League clubs, which they also preferred for

the opportunity to play alongside players such as Willie Mays and Jackie Robinson. Largely as a result of this trend, the National League eventually gained a dominance over the American League that is still unquestioned a quarter of a century later.

The Dodgers won 22 of their first 24 games in 1955, opening up a 9½-game lead by the end of the season's first month. Clinching the flag on 8 September, the earliest date in National League history, they never dropped out of first place, and finished 13½ games ahead of the second-place Braves. Don Newcombe had a 20-5 season and Roy Campanella joined baseball's elite few who have won three Most Valuable Player Awards. Featuring Gil Hodges, Carl Furillo, Jackie Robinson, Pee Wee Reese and RBI leader Duke Snider, the Dodgers as a team hit a total of 201 home runs.

Best of all, the Bums won the World Series. After losing every one of their first seven contests, including five to the Yankees, in 1955 the Dodgers won what was to be their first and last World Series as the Brooklyn Dodgers. The deciding seventh game featured a famous play by Sandy Amoros in the bottom of the sixth when, with two on, Yogi Berra sliced a line drive down the left field line. Amoros managed to catch it with a sprint that carried him into the railings, but recovered quickly enough to relay the ball to

Joseph Wilbur Adcock played outfield and first base for 17 years in the majors – with the Reds (1950-52), the Braves (1953-62), the Indians (1963), the Dodgers (1964) and the Angels (1965-66). He hit 336 homers and had a .277 batting average. He also managed Cleveland in 1967, coming in eighth.

Right: Ted Kluszewski is welcomed at the plate after his 14th home run of the 1955 season by (left to right) Wally Post, Wes Westrum and the batboy. Theodore Bernard 'Klu' Kluszewski played first base for the Reds (1947-57), the Pirates (1958-59), the Cubs (1959-60) and the Dodgers (1961). He had a lifetime batting average of .298 and hit 279 home runs.
Below: The young Henry Aaron.

Reese, who doubled up on McDougald at first. The Yankee's rally was over, and they never came close again.

Representing National League power this year was Mays with 51 homers, Kluszewski with 47, Ernie Banks with 44 and Mathews with 41. Henry Aaron had his first big year with 27 homers, 106 RBI's and a .314 average. Pittsburgh's 20-year-old Roberto Clemente, whom the Dodgers had mistakenly exposed to the draft, and who was eventually to take his place alongside Pirate greats Honus Wagner and Ralph Kiner, debuted with a modest .225.

At the annual winter meeting, National League directors voted 6 to 2 to make compulsory the wearing of protective headgear by all players when batting. Leo Durocher resigned as manager of the Giants at the end of the season to take an executive position with the National Broadcasting Company.

The Dodgers, who played seven 'home' games, one with each league rival, in Jersey City, New Jersey in 1956, as they would in 1957, sparking speculation that they would soon depart from Brooklyn permanently, took the pennant again in 1956, but only after taking the race down to the last day of the season, for the fourth time in eight years. Don Newcombe won his 27th and last victory of the regular season against the Pirates in the last game of the season to give the Dodgers the game they needed to secure the pennant from the Braves. For his performance that season, Newk was voted the first Cy Young Award, which was inaugurated at the suggestion of Commissioner Frick to recognize pitching excellence in the majors, and was also named Most Valuable Player.

The Milwaukee Braves, with annual attendance continuing above the 2 million mark, had now become serious contenders. Warren Spahn, Lew Burdette and Bob Buhl led the strong pitching staff, with Mathews, Adcock and Aaron supplying the power. Henry Aaron, by now as strong an all-round player as Willie Mays, if lacking his flamboyance, took his first batting title in 1956 with a .328 average.

Cincinnati, which the Dodgers eliminated only in the last days of the pennant race, tied the Giants' major-league home run club total record of 221, 20-year-old Frank Robinson hitting 38 home runs to take the Rookie of the Year Award with the only unanimous vote since the award's inception. Robinson's 38 homers tied the 1930 record for a rookie set by Wally Berger, and added to the established power of Reds' sluggers Kluszewski, Wally Post, Gus Bell and Ed Bailey.

The Dodgers lost the World Series to the Yankees in seven games in 1956, but not before Yankee hurler Don Larsen retired 27 Brooklyn batters in a row in the fifth game, the only perfect game in World Series history. In other landmark events, Pittsburgh first baseman Dale Long hit home runs in eight consecutive games – baseball's greatest consecutive-game home run streak – before Don Newcome stopped him

Frank Robinson when he played for Cincinnati. Robinson played, usually as an outfielder, for the Reds (1956-65), The Orioles (1966-71), the Dodgers (1972), the Angels (1973-74) and the Indians (1974-76). Hitting .294, he also belted 586 home runs. When he became the manager of the Indians in 1975, he was the first black man to manage in the major leagues. This Hall of Famer was voted the Most Valuable Player in the National League in 1961 and the Most Valuable Player in the American League in 1966.

Dale Long connects for a home run at Forbes Field in Pittsburgh. The catcher is Roy Campanella of the Dodgers and the umpire is Lee Ballafant. Richard Dale Long, with his .267 batting average, bounced around quite a bit in his 10-year career. He played first base for the Pirates (1951), the Browns (1951), the Pirates again (1955-57), the Cubs (1957-59), the Giants (1960), the Yankees (1960), the Senators (1961-62) and the Yankees again (1962-63).

on 29 May. On 1 October, the Major League Baseball Players' Association was formally organized in New York.

The Braves, losing the pennant by one game in 1956, bounced back hard in 1957 to take the flag, finishing eight games ahead of the second-place Cardinals while setting a new National League attendance record of 2,215,404. The best a somewhat aging Dodger team could do was third, the first time in nine years the Bums fell below first or second. Warren Spahn pitched his eighth 20-game year, and was ably assisted by Braves Lew Burdette and Bob Buhl, a specialist at beating the Dodgers. Henry Aaron hit 44 home runs and 132 RBI's with a season average of .322, and took the MVP.

The Braves crowned their pennant by beating the Yankees in the World Series, which for the third consecutive year went to seven games. Lew Burdette won three of those for the Braves, two of them shutouts, and Aaron polished his MVP crown by hitting .393 for the Series.

The Cardinals' Stan Musial, now 36, took his seventh and last National League batting title with a .351 average. This was the fifth time The Man topped .350, a feat equalled in the National League only by Wagner, Hornsby and Paul Waner. Jackie Robinson, who broke the color line with the Dodgers ten years earlier, retired before the start of the season rather than be traded to the Giants.

But the real news of the 1957 season was the announcement that the Giants and the Dodgers were moving to the West Coast. Startling as the Braves' move to Milwaukee had been, their move had kept the National League east of the Mississippi, where it had always been. Milwaukee had even hosted a National League club in 1878.

Until the early 1950s, organized baseball was really only practical in the cities clustered in the East and Midwest, where travel by train was neither overly expensive nor time-consuming. But air travel and income from radio and television made franchise shifts possible to clubs which faced declining attendance in antiquated ball parks in deteriorating urban settings. The Braves' spectacular success – in 1957 they led the league in attendance – convinced beleaguered club owners that greener pastures did indeed exist.

The Giants, in New York since 1883, announced on 19 August 1957 that they had decided to play their last game at the Polo Grounds on 29 September and move to San Francisco. The reasons for moving out of their outmoded ball park were classic, particularly with

respect to attendance, which had fallen from 1,155,067 in their 1954 championship year to 629,179 in 1956. When President Horace Stoneham was asked if he felt bad about taking the Giants away from the kids of New York, he replied, 'I feel bad about the kids, but I haven't seen too many of their fathers lately.'

On 8 October the Brooklyn Dodgers confirmed years of persistent rumors by announcing that they too had decided to move west, to Los Angeles. Brooklyn had no problems with attendance, although Ebbets Field had become impossible, but owner O'Malley was fascinated by the prospect of the profits to be reaped by planting his team in one of the

Fans chase their Giants into the clubhouse after the game of 30 September 1957 as the Pirates trot up the steps at left. This was the Giants' last appearance at the Polo Grounds before their move to San Francisco.

nation's most affluent, rapidly growing metropolitan areas. It was O'Malley, in fact, who finally convinced Giant owner Stoneham to move west, partly out of fear that the league might not approve a single franchise shift to the West Coast.

The New York clubs' dreams of riches panned out in 1958 with the Dodgers hosting 1,845,566 fans at the Los Angeles Memorial Coliseum, almost 40,000 more than their best at Ebbets Field, and the Giants drawing 1,272,625 at the much smaller Seals Stadium. On 18 April, Los Angeles set a new single-day attendance mark for the league when 78,672 fans came to see the Dodgers play the Giants in the first major-league game ever played on the West Coast.

Despite the cheers of their new fans, the Dodgers fell to seventh place in 1958, only two games out of the cellar, due in part to a pre-season automobile accident which left their three-time MVP Hall of Famer star catcher Roy Campanella permanently paralyzed. The Giants fell to third, 12 games behind the league-leading Braves, although Willie Mays hit his best-ever .347 and Rookie of the Year first baseman Orlando Cepeda hit .312. Ernie Banks of Chicago hit 47 home runs to set a record for shortstop and win the MVP Award.

Three of 1958's 20-game winners – Warren Spahn, Lew Burdette, and Bob Friend of Pittsburgh – were with the pennant-repeating Braves, who finished 8 games ahead of the second-place Pirates. After taking a 3-1 lead, the Braves dropped the World Series to the Yankees.

The main event on the diamond in 1959 was the pitching of 12 perfect innings by Pittsburgh's Harvey

Below: Orlando Manuel 'The Baby Bull' or 'Cha-Cha' Cepeda played for a number of teams from 1958 to 1974. He hit 379 home runs and carried a .297 batting average.

Haddix. For most of his 14-year career an unremarkable pitcher, on 29 May the 34-year-old southpaw established a major-league record by retiring the first 36 Braves he faced. These included Aaron, Mathews and Adcock, on a Milwaukee team that was undoubtedly the hardest-hitting in the league.

Harvey saw his first man reach base when third baseman Don Hoak made a bad throw after fielding a grounder hit by Felix Mantilla in the bottom of the 13th. Mathews sacrificed Mantilla to second, Aaron was purposely walked, and Adcock, whom Haddix had already struck out twice, hit a home run just over the right-center field fence. Confused base-running by the Braves voided two runs, but Haddix lost baseball's best pitched game, 1-0.

The 1959 pennant race was a three-way fight between the Dodgers, the Braves and the Giants, with the Giants leading by two games into the final week. As the Giants slipped, the Braves and the Dodgers added steam, ending the season tied, and forcing the third pennant playoff in National League history.

The Dodgers, in their third playoff appearance, won the first game in Milwaukee and wrapped up the best two-out-of-three in the next game in Los Angeles with a heroic three-run rally in the bottom of the ninth, and another in the bottom of the 12th. Their dramatic comeback from seventh to first place in the second year of their move west was rewarded by record-breaking crowds at their three home games in a World Series they won from the White Sox in six games. The Series games at the Los Angeles Coliseum drew 92,394, 92,650 and finally 92,796, the largest crowds in World Series history, topping the 86,288 mark set at Cleveland in 1948.

Both Warren Spahn and Lew Burdette again won 20 games for the Braves, and Henry Aaron took the league batting title with .355, his highest average ever. For Spahn, now 38, this was his tenth 20-game year. Chicago's Ernie Banks became the first in league history to take the MVP two years running, and Giant Willie McCovey, batting .354, Rookie of the Year.

Events on the playing field in 1959 were to a considerable extent overshadowed by the attempt of Branch Rickey's Continental League to become the third major league, and by Congressional hearings into the laws governing professional baseball. The failure of Congress to pass a bill sponsored by Senator Estes Kefauver of Tennessee effectively killed Rickey's idea on the drawing board, but in its failure sowed the seeds for the first expansion of the major leagues in 60 years. The American League would increase to ten clubs in 1961, and the National League, bowing to public demand, would expand to accommodate America's growing love of baseball in 1962.

Left: Willie McCovey takes a swing. Willie Lee 'Stretch' McCovey played most of his career at first base for the Giants and was a prodigious home run hitter who was the Most Valuable Player in the National League in 1969.

CHAPTER SIX

The Unpredictable Decade

I didn't think our pitchers were all that good!

Hank Bauer, Manager of the Orioles, 1966

The 1960s have come to stand as one of the most unsettling and divisive decades in the history of America, and in some ways professional major league baseball did reflect at least some of the dynamism of the period. By the end of the 1950s, for instance, television was already having an impact on the development of major league baseball. For one thing, television was creating a new and more widespread public for major league baseball – a public that lived far beyond traditional population centers that had supported baseball teams. As millions of Americans in the Far West and the South began to enjoy the games on television, they began to wish they might have a team closer to home to support. A new group of entrepreneurs also began to consider owning a baseball club; it was a potentially profitable enterprise, and beyond that a major league club was for both the owner and the home town a matter of prestige and just plain fun.

The failure of the Continental League only brought the issue of more teams for more cities to a head. So it was that in 1962 the National League – following the lead taken by the American League in 1961 – added two new teams: the New York Mets and the Houston Colt 45s. (It would be 1965 before the Houston team would exchange this rather awkward name for the Astros.) This same year – and for the same reason that the American League had done so in 1961 when it added two teams – the National League increased the number of games played for a full season from 154 to 162.

Then, in 1969 – the same year, as it happened, that Bowie Kuhn took over as the new Commissioner of Baseball – both leagues expanded to 12 teams. The new National League teams were the San Diego Padres and the Montreal Expos – the first major league club outside the United States, and further testimony to the spread of baseball's public. In expanding to 12 teams, each league also split itself into two six-team divisions, Eastern and Western. At the time, some 'purists' complained that this was a thinly disguised move to four leagues, but very quickly the new teams became identified with their respective leagues. Although the standings on any given day called attention to the divisions, most fans retained a strong sense of identity with either the National League or the American League.

For the National League, this expansion to 12 teams proved to be the limit: the National League would not follow the lead of the American League, which expanded to 14 teams in 1977. Likewise, the shifting of teams from city to city that continued in the American League well into the 1970s ended in 1966 for the National League when the Milwaukee Braves moved to Atlanta. With this move, the National League remained 'in place' at least into the 1990s if not for all time. But the National League could not become too smug about its traditionalism: after all, it had been the Boston Braves' move to Milwaukee in 1953 that had begun the whole post-war shifting of clubs – and the Braves only moved from Milwaukee because they had experienced a loss in attendance.

There would be other developments in the 1960s that, if not necessarily linked to the dynamism of society at large, did seem to suggest that organized baseball was at least trying to keep up with the times. In 1969, for instance, the major leagues adopted two changes in the rules of the game because there were fears that pitchers had been gaining so much control over the hitters that the sport would lose fans. Whether this was a concern generated by the rising prominence of television was debatable: true fans, it has been said, can enjoy a tight pitchers' duel on any given day at the ballpark as much as a slugfest, while on the small screen a slugfest undoubtedly seems more exciting.

The argument that the pitchers were becoming too dominant, in any case, seemed somewhat questionable in the decade that would witness assaults on several of the major all-time records by hitters. It would be in 1961 that Roger Maris hit 61 home runs, while Henry Aaron and several others continued to hit home runs at such a pace that a number of players would break into the charmed circle of 3000 lifetime hits and 500 home runs. True, Sandy Koufax, Bob Gibson, Denny McLain and some other pitchers would set some amazing records. But any decade that began with a World Series that had the Pirates defeating the Yankees and ended with a Series that saw the Mets defeating the Orioles had no cause to fear that baseball was becoming too predictable.

When the 1960 season began, no one would have picked the Pittsburgh Pirates to win in the National League. The Milwaukee Braves seemed to be the team

Below: Richard Morrow 'Dick' Groat played shortstop for 14 years in the National League with Pittsburgh (1952-62), St Louis (1963-65), Philadelphia (1966-67) and San Francisco (1967). Voted Most Valuable Player in the National League in 1960, he had a lifetime batting average of .286.

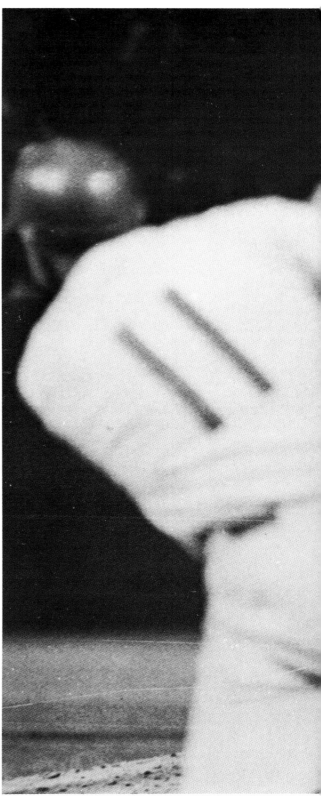

to beat, what with Warren Spahn pitching himself and Eddie Mathews and Hank Aaron hitting themselves into the record books. Or there were those perennial threats, the Dodgers, fresh from their 1959 World Series win over the Chicago White Sox. The Dodgers had Wally Moon and Maury Wills and the league's leading strikeout pitcher, Don Drysdale; they also had a still promising pitcher, Sandy Koufax, who by the end of the season, with only an 8-13 record, would have given signs of something special; Koufax struck out 197 and he led the league in fewest hits per nine innings. But the best the Dodgers could do in 1960 was fourth place.

The Pirates, meanwhile, neither on paper nor on

the field were a team of superstars. But Roberto Clemente hit .314 and shortstop Dick Groat came through with a .325 to take the league batting title (and the Most Valuable Player award); for pitchers, Pittsburgh had Vernon Law, who won 20 while losing nine; Bob Friend, who won 18; Wilmer 'Vinegar Bend' Mizell, just purchased from the Cardinals, who won 13; and Elroy Face for relief. And under the savvy management of Danny Murtaugh, the Pirates took first place, leaving the Braves seven games behind.

The Yankees who took the American League that year were hardly the powerhouse of other years, but they had Mickey Mantle, Roger Maris and Bill Skowron, and Whitey Ford for pitching. Furthermore,

the Yankees were a team used to taking the World Series while the Pirates hadn't appeared in one since 1927 – when the Yankees, in fact, wiped them out in four straight. So most people probably would have picked the Yankees for 1960. And indeed, looking only at the stats, the Yankees seem to have cleaned up: the Yankees set new Series records with 55 runs scored (vs only 27 for the Pirates), 91 hits, including 27 extra-base hits, and a .338 team batting average (vs .256 for the Pirates). Yet with some well-timed hits, and some tight pitching by Vernon Law and Elroy Face, the Pirates forced the Series into the seventh game on 13 October. The starting pitchers, Bob Turley for the Yankees and Vernon Law for the

Above: Donald Scott 'Big D' Drysdale pitched for the Dodgers for 14 years (1956-69), both in Brooklyn and Los Angeles. He won 209 games with a 2.95 earned run average and a strikeout record of 2486. This Hall of Famer won the Cy Young Award in 1962.

Above: Maury Wills steals another base against the Giants. Shortstop Wills, the MVP in the National League in 1962, had 2134 career hits, carried a .281 batting average, and stole 586 bases (104 of them in the 1962 season).
Right: Vernon Sanders 'Deacon' Law pitched for the Pirates (1950-67). His ERA was 3.77 and he beat the Yankees twice in the 1960 World Series.

Pirates, were soon knocked out and the game see-sawed back and forth until it went into the ninth inning, where the Yankees tied it up, 9-9. In the bottom of the ninth, Ralph Terry was by then pitching for the Yankees; Bill Mazeroski, the Pirates second baseman, connected with Terry's second pitch and sent it over the ivy-covered left-field wall of Forbes Field to climax one of the most exciting Series in memory.

The 1961 season turned out to be memorable in another way – with its various records set. Of course the one that dominated everyone's attention was the race by Mantle and Maris to at least tie Babe Ruth's major league record of 60 homers in a season (1927); as everyone knows, Maris broke that record with his 61st homer on the last game of the 162-game season. Meanwhile, over in the National League, some other records were being set in 1961. The Phillies, alas, lost 23 games in a row between 29 July and 20 August – the longest losing streak in modern major-league baseball. Willie Mays hit four homers on 30 April. Warren Spahn, pitching for the Milwaukee Braves, got his second no-hitter on 28 April and his 300th win on 11 August (only the third in the National League, after Mathewson and Alexander). Maury Wills, the Dodger shortstop, stole 50 bases – the best in the league since 1923.

In the National League's pennant race, it was between the Dodgers and the Cincinnati Reds. The Dodgers had strong pitching from Don Drysdale, Johnny Podres and Stan Williams, but the most amazing performance was that of Sandy Koufax: he found his control this year and pitched 269 strikeouts, walking only 96, in 256 innings to gain an 18-13 record. But the Reds had not only pitching – Joey Jay (21 wins) and Jim O'Toole (19 wins) – but also solid hitting from Vada Pinson (.343) and Frank Robinson (.323). No one gave the Reds much chance, though, in the Series, where the Yankees were regarded as one of the most powerful teams since their 1927 team with Ruth and Gehrig. And indeed, the Reds were knocked out, four games to one, although more by Yankee pitching than the expected powerhitting. There are some seasons that just have to be accepted and 1961 was such a one for the National League.

The 1962 season, however, proved more eventful. To begin with, the League added two new teams – as the American League had done in 1961 – so there was now a National League team back in New York, the Mets, while Houston had its first team, the Colt .45s – which would be renamed the Astros in 1965. Under their manager, Casey Stengel, who had been dropped by the Yankees in 1960, the Mets won the hearts of many fans but also lost many games – 120, in fact, out of 162, the most games ever lost by a modern major league team. The season also witnessed some other more inspiring records. Stan Musial, on 19 May, got his 3431st hit, taking over first place (from Honus Wagner) in the National League. And Maury Wills overtook and tied Ty Cobb's 47-year-old record of 96 stolen bases in 156 games (Detroit had played two extra games because of ties that year) and then went on to steal 104, then a major-league record.

Wills' base stealing feats helped to spark the Dodgers team, which also included such standout performances as Tommy Davis' .346 batting average and 153 RBI's and Don Drysdale's 25-9 record. Sandy Koufax tied his own (1959) and Bob Feller's (1938) record of 18 strikeouts in nine innings but a circulation problem in his pitching hand kept him out of action in the last half of the season. The result was that the Dodgers ended up on the last day in a tie for first place with their arch enemies, the Giants. These Giants had a total of 204 home runs, thanks to players like Mays, McCovey, Alou and Cepeda. In the playoff – the fourth in National League history, all of which the Dodgers had been involved in – the first two games were split. The Dodgers went into the ninth inning with a 4-2 lead, but before three Dodger pitchers could retire the Giants, they had taken the lead, 6-4. And that was it for the Dodgers of 1962.

Now the Giants turned around to face another

Below: Casey Stengel when he was manager of the rag-tag New York Mets – 'Can't anybody here play this game?'

Above left: Ron Perranoski warms up. Perranoski pitched for 13 years in the big leagues (1961-73) – with the Dodgers, Twins, Tigers and Angels – maintaining a 2.79 ERA.

Above right: Stan Musial of the Cardinals comes into second base as a very young Pete Rose of the Reds looks on. This was Rose's first year in the majors (1963), and he won the Rookie of the Year Award.

traditional rival – the New York Yankees: it would be the seventh Series these teams had played, although the previous six had been subway affairs. The teams seemed about evenly matched: the Yankees had Whitey Ford and Ralph Terry – but the Giants had Juan Marichal and Jack Sanford; the Yankees had Mantle and Maris, but the Giants had Willie Mays and Orlando Cepeda. And right through the first six games, the teams did indeed stay even. In the seventh game, at Candlestick Park, Terry faced Sanford, and going into the ninth inning the only score was a run by the Yankees in the fifth inning. In the bottom of the ninth, with two out and Felipe Alou on third, Willie McCovey came to bat, and you can be sure that every-

one watching the game was talking about Mazeroski's homer of 1960. McCovey took Terry's pitch and lined it toward right field – but this time second baseman Bobby Richardson caught the ball. The Yankees had won, 1-0, and were the World Champions for the second year in a row.

But baseball is the classic 'Wait till next year!' sport, and never was this truer than in 1963. For one, the Dodgers came back from their humiliating defeat by the Giants at the end of 1962 and took the National League pennant. The Giants, despite the fine pitching of Marichal (25-8), simply couldn't stand up to the Dodgers and the Cardinals this year. Neither could the Milwaukee Braves, despite another fine season by

Koufax struck out 15 Yankees (breaking Carl Erskine's Series record of 14, set in 1953, on the exact same date), and in the second game Podres, with some help from Perranoski in the bottom of the ninth, beat the Yankees 4-1. In the third game, Jim Bouton gave up only four hits and one run, but that was good enough for Drysdale to win 1-0 on only three hits. In the fourth game, it was Koufax against Ford again, and the game remained tied, 1-1, going into the seventh inning; then Yankee first baseman Joe Pepitone missed a throw (he blamed it on the wall of white shirted fans he was facing!) and the Dodgers had a man on third; a deep outfield fly allowed him to score, and even with only two fair hits, this was enough to give the Dodgers the game, 2-1, and the Series.

The 1963 season was also notable for National League fans as it was the last for Stan Musial as a player. His final hit of the season came on 29 September, and as number 3630 it would stand as the league record for many years. Watching Musial that day was the Cincinnati Red's rookie second baseman, 21-year-old Pete Rose, who would have reason to remember the occasion.

And the Phillies would long remember the 1964 season. They had come breezing into the last two weeks of the season with what seemed like a safe 6½-game lead. Then, beginning on 20 September, they lost 10 straight games. Well, teams had gone into tailspins before – the Phillies themselves had done so in 1950, losing seven of their last nine, but they had just managed to pull out in first place. But in 1964, while the Phillies went cold, the Cardinals went hot: they won eight in a row – and by the last day, the Cardinals had taken the pennant with a one-game lead.

Juan Marichal – one of the toughest pitchers of all time. Juan Antonio Sanchez 'Manito' or 'The Dominican Dandy' Marichal pitched for the Giants (1960-73), the Red Sox (1974) and the Dodgers (1975). His record was 243-142 and he had a fine 2.89 earned run average with 2303 strikeouts and 52 shutouts, which got him elected to the Hall of Fame.

the 42-year-old Warren Spahn: his 23-7 record was his 13th (if last) 20-game season. And in the end, the Cardinals couldn't hold off the Dodgers. The Dodgers had a couple of power hitters in Frank Howard and Tommy Davis, but mostly they relied on the fast and clever base running by Maury Wills, Willie Davis and Jim Gilliam. In addition to another solid season from Don Drysdale and Johnny Podres and fine relief from Ron Perranoski, the Dodgers got an extraordinary season from Sandy Koufax: a 25-5 record, an earned run average of only 1.88, 306 strikeouts (almost one per inning), and 11 shutouts.

And this year the Dodgers got another chance to avenge themselves on the Yankees. In the first game,

Above: Nolan Ryan, the master of strikeouts. Lynn Nolan Ryan began his career in 1966 with the Mets, who traded him to the California Angels in 1972. He went to Houston in 1980, and to the Texas Rangers in 1989, where he set the all-time mark for career strikeouts. He retired four years later with 5714 strikeouts and an unprecedented seven no-hitters.

Actually, the 1964 season yielded several memorable occasions for the National League. One was on 21 June, when Jim Bunning of these same Phillies pitched a perfect game against the New York Mets – the first perfect game in the National League in modern baseball. And only a few weeks before, the Mets had been involved in another memorable game: on the night of 31 May, the Mets played the Giants in a doubleheader, and as expected, the Giants took the first, 5-3; but the second game went on and on – 23 innings, in fact, until the Giants won that, too, 8-6 – and the fans had been treated, if that's the word, to nine hours 52 minutes of baseball, a modern record. Everyone over a certain age who was in New York City that night can recall how the whole town buzzed as the game went on into the early hours of the morning.

But the Cardinals were no laughing matter that year. They had solid hitters in Dick Groat, formerly with the Pirates, Ken Boyer, Bill White, Tim McCarver and Curt Flood; they also had acquired a new outfielder in a swap with the Cubs, a Lou Brock, who could run – and steal – as well as hit. And they had a fastball pitcher and hardball player in Bob Gibson. Still, the Yankees, with their fifth straight American League pennant, had to be the favorites. And with Mickey Mantle hitting record-breaking home runs, it

did seem that the Yankees were going to overpower the Cardinals. But the Cardinals never gave up and they took the Yankees into a seventh game. Gibson pitched and gave up homers to Mantle, Clete Boyer and Phil Linz, but his teammates gave him a couple runs more to spare, and the Cardinals won the Series, 7-5.

But in 1965, the Cardinals couldn't hold their own against the two traditional rivals, the Dodgers and Giants; both teams got hot in September – amazingly so, with the Dodgers winning 13 in a row and the Giants winning 14 in a row. Willie Mays hit 52 home runs, but this wasn't enough to win the pennant, for the Dodgers moved into the lead under their superb pitching and ended up in first place by two games. Don Drysdale had a 23-12 record while Koufax had 26-8 – between them they struck out almost 600 opponents. Koufax had some other amazing stats, including 382 strikeouts, a new major league record that would hold until Nolan Ryan struck out 383 in 1973; and Koufax joined that most exclusive of all major league clubs when he pitched a perfect game against the Cubs on 9 September. (The Cubs pitcher, Bob Hendley, gave up only one hit, so the Cubs lost only by 1-0.)

So it was that the Dodgers once again found themselves in a World Series – for the 12th time, in fact – but facing a team that was in it for the first time, the Minnesota Twins (although these Twins were actually old Washington Senators). The Twins had made their way into the Series with such heavy hitters as Harmon Killebrew, Bob Allison, Don Minchner and Tony Oliva. The Dodgers, however, had fewer home runs than any other major league team in 1965, but relied instead on putting together steady base hits and smart baserunning: Maury Wills, for instance, batted only .286 but he stole 94 bases. And then, to be sure, there were Koufax and Drysdale. When the Series opened, it looked as though the Twins' big bats were going to prove stronger than the big arms: the Twins beat Drysdale in the opener, 8-2, and then knocked Koufax off the mound in the second and went on to win, 5-1. Back at Los Angeles, the Dodgers rebounded and with a combination of hitting, pitching and baserunning, they swept all three games there. The Twins took the sixth game, so the Series once more went into the seventh game. But here is where the Dodgers' depth paid off. Minnesota pitched Jim Kaat, good, but not a match for Koufax at his best: Koufax gave up only three hits and kept the Twins from ever reaching home, shutting them down, 2-0, and giving Walt Alston his fourth World Championship.

Once in a while major league baseball needs a season with no particular fireworks or spectacular surprises, and 1966 was such a season. It was a time of foundation-laying, of consolidation. The Mets, for instance, brought up a 19-year-old fastball pitcher, Nolan Ryan, while the Chicago Cubs acquired a promising young pitcher named Ferguson Jenkins from the Phillies. Meanwhile, the Cincinnati Reds had let their ace batter, Frank Robinson, go because he was asking more money than they thought he was worth: he jumped the league and went over to the Baltimore Orioles, who soon discovered he was worth every penny. The Los Angeles Dodgers made no such mistake, though, when their ace pitchers, Sandy Koufax and Don Drysdale, both held out for what was then regarded as Big Money – over $100,000 – and got it.

The National League race was fairly tight, right up to the end. The Pirates looked like they might take it,

what with such hitters as Matty Alou – whose .342 was the league's high – and Willie Stargell, Donn Clendenon and Roberto Clemente (whose all-round play made him the most valuable player) but the team lacked pitchers. The Braves had just settled in Atlanta this year, after 13 years in Milwaukee, but despite Hank Aaron's continuing home run production, the Braves could do no better than fifth place. And the Giants, despite the fine pitching of Juan Marichel (25-6) and Gaylord Perry (21-8) could do no better than second place, 1½ games behind the Dodgers.

Yes, the Dodgers did it again, although not with much to spare. Drysdale had an off year with 13-6, but Koufax had a brilliant season, with a 27-9 record and

an ERA of 1.73. Claude Osteen, Ron Perranoski and rookie Don Sutton also pitched in, while the batting and fielding of such as Maury Wills, Willie Davis, Lou Johnson, Jim Lefebvre and Tommy Davis gave them the winning edge. The Dodgers went into the World Series the favorites over the American League winner, the Baltimore Orioles. But the Orioles' pitching staff – Dave McNally, Jim Palmer, young Wally Bunker and aging Moe Drabowsky – shut down the Dodgers (the last 33 innings the Dodgers went scoreless) and took the Series in four straight. It was not only an ignominious end to the season, it was the end of an era for the Dodgers. Tommy Davis and Maury Wills would be traded away that winter, while Sandy

Above: Johnny Podres delivers a fastball. John Joseph Podres played for the Dodgers, both in Brooklyn and Los Angeles (1953-66), the Tigers (1966-67) and the Padres (1969). He won 148 games and had an earned run average of 3.67.

Above: A young Tom Seaver on the mound. George Thomas Seaver pitched for the Mets from 1967 to 1977, when he was let go to the Reds and then the Mets again and then, through an apparent front office error, he was claimed by the White Sox. Voted Rookie of the Year in 1967, he has won the Cy Young Award three times.

Koufax, who had long been bothered by painful arthritis in his left elbow, announced he was retiring. He was only 31, and in his last five seasons he had a 111-34 record, but the doctors had warned him he would suffer permanent injury if he continued. Many students of the game would claim that Koufax would go down as one of the great left-handed pitchers of modern baseball.

The 1966 season had been one in which the predictable had happened during the regular season, what with the Dodgers winning the National League;

the 1967 season was full of surprises, what with the St Louis Cardinals coming back from a sixth-place finish in 1966 to take both the National League pennant and the World Series. How this came about is the stuff of baseball history. To begin with, the Dodgers of 1966 were virtually wiped out by a series of retirements and trades; although the rest of the league was not unhappy to be liberated from Koufax's control – the league's batting average rose from .249 in 1966 to .256 in 1967 – the Dodgers finished in eighth place.

Meanwhile, some other National League teams

were on the rise. The Chicago Cubs had their hot young pitcher, Ferguson Jenkins, acquired from the Phillies in 1966; Jenkins gave the Cubs the first of his seven 20-game seasons in 1967. The Mets had their own promising young pitcher, one George Thomas Seaver, who had been picked out of a hat the year before. Seaver had been signed to a $50,000 bonus contract by the Braves, but because he had signed before his class, at the University of Southern California, had graduated, a violation of organized baseball's agreement, Seaver had been declared a free agent; the commissioner's way of resolving this was to have the teams that wanted to negotiate with Seaver place their names in a hat; the New York Mets won the draw, and after one year in the Mets' farm system, Tom Seaver came up to New York and pitched 16 victories in this first season, 1967 (and became Rookie of the Year).

Left: The handsome and articulate Sandy Koufax tried his hand at baseball broadcasting.
Below: Orlando Cepeda takes a hefty swing.

Hall of Famer Red Schoendienst ready to throw. Primarily a second baseman, Schoendienst played for the Cardinals, the Giants and the Braves. He then managed the Cardinals from 1965 to 1976, winning two pennants and one World Series. He batted .289 during his career, getting 2449 hits.

But none of this was enough to stop the Cardinals. They had made their own wily deals, having acquired Orlando Cepeda, the first baseman, from the San Francisco Giants, and Roger Maris, the Yankee who had been unhappy in the glare of publicity ever since he had hit his record-breaking 61 home runs in 1961. By 15 July, the Cardinals had a lead of four games, when in that day's game against the Pirates, the Cardinals' star pitcher, Bob Gibson, had his right leg fractured by a line drive by Roberto Clemente. That seemed to mark the end of the Cardinals, but their former relief pitcher, Nelson Briles, replaced Gibson in the starting rotation, and Briles and the rest of the team did so well – Cepeda hit .325 and drove 111 runs – that they took the pennant almost two weeks before the season ended, leaving San Francisco 10½ games behind by the end.

Bob Gibson had returned to active duty in September and was in fine form by the time the World Series came round. And if the Cardinals were somewhat surprised to find themselves there, their opponents, the Boston Red Sox, were even more astonished to be playing in the Series. To counter Gibson, the Red Sox had Jim Lonborg, but he had been forced to pitch the final game of the season, when Boston clinched the pennant, so he could not pitch the opener. Gibson won that with a six-hitter, then pitched the Cardinals to their third win in the fourth game with a five-hit shutout. The showdown came in the seventh game, but Gibson had had three days of rest, Lonborg only two; Gibson pitched a three-hitter and the Cardinals got to Lonborg and won the game 7-2. The Cardinals also owed a lot to Lou Brock's hitting and base-running – he set a series record by stealing seven bases.

The Cardinals' triumph in 1967 also represented a repeat and final performance for one of the great duets of National League history – that of Red Schoendienst and Stan Musial. For ten years, from 1946 through 1955, these two were virtually inseparable from the Cardinals and from each other. Schoendienst had become the manager of the Cardinals in 1964, and Musial had become the club's general manager in 1966, and their World Championship in 1967 was a fitting climax to their years of collaboration. In December 1967, Musial resigned from the Cardinals and retired permanently from organized baseball to devote himself to his business interests.

But the Cardinals by no means retired and in 1968 they came right back and took the National League pennant for the second year in a row, with the San Francisco Giants in second place (for the fourth consecutive year), nine games behind. But that does not begin to tell the story that made the 1968 season so distinctive, that made it come to be known as 'The Year of the Pitcher.' One of the most extraordinary feats was that of the American League's Detroit Tiger, Denny McLain; his 31-6 record made him the first major leaguer to win 30 games since Dizzy Dean had done so in 1934. But the Cardinals' Bob Gibson achieved his own series of feats that are equally astounding: his earned run average was 1.12, the lowest in major league history (breaking the National League record of 1.22, set by Grover Cleveland Alexander in 1915, and the major league mark of 1.14, set by Walter Johnson in 1913); Gibson also won 15 games in a row, and pitched 13 shutouts; no wonder that Gibson won both the league's Most Valuable Player award and the Cy Young award.

But the whole season was dominated by outstanding pitching. Don Drysdale of the Los Angeles Dodgers pitched six consecutive shutouts (breaking Doc White's 64-year-old major league record) that included 58⅔ scoreless innings in a row (which broke Walter Johnson's record of 56, set in 1913). Juan Marichal of the San Francisco Giants had a 26-9 record that would have gained him far more recognition in any other season – but this always seemed to be Marichal's fate, to be eclipsed by more spectacular pitchers while he was steadily piling up a superb career. The Mets' Tom Seaver won 16 for his second year in a row. Altogether, there were 185 shutouts pitched in the National League alone – a record for any league's season – while the league's batting average was held to .243. Yet Pete Rose of the Cincinnati Reds hit .335 and got 210 hits, while Willie Mays raised his home runs total to 587, putting him in second place behind Babe Ruth.

The Cardinals confronted the Detroit Tigers in the World Series in what was assumed would be a duel between Gibson and McClain. In the first game, Gibson had 17 strikeouts, a World Series record, gave up five hits, and the Cardinals won 4-0. McLain was driven from the game in the fifth inning. But in the second game, the Tigers produced an unexpected winner in Mickey Lolich, who gave up six hits as the Tigers won, 8-1. The Cards took the next two games – Gibson taking the fourth, his seventh straight series win, a major league record – but Lolich led the Tigers to a victory in the fifth game, and McLain returned to form in the sixth game, with the Tigers winning 13-1.

So in the end, the season came down once again to one game, and it was Lolich against Gibson this time. The score was 0-0 in the seventh inning, when Gibson gave up two singles and then Northrup hit what should have been a routine out; instead, the usually flawless Curt Flood misjudged it and two runs scored; the Tigers went on to win the game, 4-1, and become the World Champions. Lou Brock of the Cardinals, however, hit .464 and stole seven bases, and tied seven series records for batting and baserunning.

So concerned were the powers-that-be that the pitchers were shutting down the action – and thus driving away the fans – that the rules committee of

Pete Rose questions a call. Peter Edward 'Charlie Hustle' Rose began his career in Cincinnati in 1963, where he was named Rookie of the Year. He moved to Philadelphia in 1979, then to Montreal and finally made a triumphant return to the Reds as player-manager in 1984. In 1985 he set the record for the most career hits of anyone in baseball – breaking Ty Cobb's record of 4191.

organized baseball voted in two major changes after the 1968 season ended. The height of the pitching mound was lowered from 15 inches to 10 inches – to strip pitchers of some of their 'superiority' – and the strike zone was reduced (from its longstanding shoulders-to-knee) down to the armpit to top of the knee. Whether such changes would seriously affect the game was argued intensely at first, but they soon seemed to become just two more factors among many variables, in a sport that often seemed to depend on unpredictables and incalculables as much as pitchers' statistics.

And never was this more so than in the 1969 season. When the season began, the biggest topic of speculation was the expanded 12-team leagues with two divisions, Eastern and Western. The pressure to add more teams had been building for some time, and the final plans were agreed upon at the end of the 1968 season. The National League added the San Diego Padres and the Montreal Expos and then divided itself as follows: The Eastern Division, with Chicago Cubs, Montreal Expos, New York Mets, Philadelphia Phillies, Pittsburgh Pirates and St Louis Cardinals; and the Western Division, with the Atlanta Braves, Cincinnati Reds, Houston Astros, Los Angeles Dodgers, San Diego Padres, and San Francisco Giants. Each league held to the 162-games with schedules that had a team playing all of the other 11 teams but more of their games against those in their division; there would be playoffs

between the divisional winners to decide the pennant winner and World Series representative.

And so the 1969 season began with this new format, and even though each of the new clubs was allowed to draft 30 players from the rosters of the other 10 teams in their league, it was accepted that these expansion teams had little chance against the older, established teams. Why, one only had to look at the New York Mets, one of the expansion teams of 1962; in its seven years in the league, the team had never finished above ninth place, and their very name had become synonymous with amateurish, bumbling play. Yet the individual Mets certainly didn't regard themselves as any less professional or hard-playing than any other major leaguers; yes, they made their share of errors (and perhaps a few extraordinary bloopers) but they hung in there, year after year. Now, in 1969, they had as manager Gil Hodges, once a first baseman for the Brooklyn Dodgers, a man who knew how to get the most out of his young players. For these Mets were young: 21 of them were between 21 and 28 years old. And they were not especially strong in the hitting department: they ended up with a team batting average of .241, eighth in the league, and eight other teams in the league outscored the Mets. But the Mets got the hit when they needed it. In one game, Steve Carlton of the Cardinals struck out 19 Mets, but they went on to win 4-3 because Ron Swoboda hit two two-run homers.

Above: Ron Swoboda of the Mets. Ronald Allan 'Rocky' Swoboda was a journeyman outfielder for the Mets (1965–70), the Expos (1971) and the Yankees (1971–73), hitting a mere .242 and hitting 73 home runs. But he will be remembered for his work in 1969, when his miraculous catches and .467 batting average in the World Series helped so much to win the championship for New York. He later became a creditable sports commentator on television.

Opposite: The great Gil Hodges. Gilbert Raymond Hodges had managed the Senators from 1963 to 1967 and took over the lackluster Mets from 1968 to 1971. He inherited a last-place ball club and worked a miracle, leading them to the World Series championship in just two years.

runs, and Phil Niekro with his 23 wins. And the Braves did get to the Mets' pitchers. But the Mets got to the Braves pitchers even more so – 37 hits, in fact, as the Mets took the playoff in three straight, 9-5, 11-6, 7-4.

Still, many people felt, a playoff series was one thing – the World Series against the experienced Baltimore Orioles was something else. And when the Orioles took the first game, 4-1, with Tom Seaver losing to Mike Cuellar, reason seemed to have returned to the game. But Jerry Koosman gave up only two hits in the second game, and the Mets won 2-1. Then Gary Gentry and Nolan Ryan combined to lead the Mets to a 5-0 victory. In the fourth game, the Mets went into the 10th inning with the score 1-1; Jerry Grote got a double when Buford misplayed a simple fly ball, Weis was given a walk, J C Martin bunted toward the mound and the Orioles' pitcher Pete Richert threw to first but hit Martin on the wrist and the ball bounced away – allowing a winning run to score. Replay photos showed that Martin had in fact run illegally into foul territory, but it was not caught by the umpires in the field, so now the Mets had three victories. In the fifth game, the Orioles were leading 3-0 when the Mets Cleon Jones came up in the sixth

Above: Philip Henry Niekro began pitching for the Braves in 1964, when they were still in Milwaukee. He now pitches for the Yankees and registered his win number 300 in 1985 at the age of 46 – the oldest pitcher to reach that level – and it was a shutout, which made him the oldest pitcher to pitch a no-run game.
Far right: Tug McGraw and Jerry Koosman share a sandwich. Frank Edwin McGraw played for the Mets and the Phillies and Jerome Martin Koosman was also a Met. These were two of the stalwarts who, along with Tom Seaver, starred in the pitching lineup for the Miracle Mets of 1969.
Opposite top: Jerry Koosman in 1968.

What the Mets did draw on was some exceptional pitching, especially by Tom Seaver, whose 25-7 record was the best in the majors. Jerry Koosman ran up a 17-9 record, while Tug McGraw in relief saved 12 and won 9. Mostly, though, the Mets of 1969 drew on some uncalculable spirit, some energy. The Chicago Cubs were leading the Eastern Division almost all season and were outhitting and outscoring the Mets; by 13 August, the Mets were 9½ games behind the Cubs and most smart money would have declared the Mets out for another season. But something happened. By 10 September, the Mets had sneaked into the lead; Seaver and Koosman pitched 19 victories in August and September; the Mets won 38 of their last 49 games; meanwhile, the Cubs collapsed, and when the season ended, they were in second place, 8 games behind the Miraculous Mets.

But now there were two divisions, and the Mets had to go into the league playoffs against the Western Division winner, the Atlanta Braves. The Braves had hit their way to the top against a lot of strong competition and were favored to take the Mets handily: after all, these Braves had Hank Aaron, with his 44 home inning; when the umpire failed to agree that he had been hit on the foot by one pitch, Jones proved it by showing that there was shoe polish on the ball; he then scored when Clendenon hit a homer; in the seventh inning, Al Weis hit another homer and the game was tied. In the eighth inning, the Mets got two doubles, but Baltimore made two throwing errors and the Mets took the lead, 5-3. It held – and the Mets were the World Champions.

The New York Mets fans were not the only Americans to become almost delirious with this incredible climax to the season. The whole country had become somewhere between intrigued and obsessed by this 'team of destiny.' And this in a summer that saw the first human beings walk on the moon. It was no coincidence that the National League set a new attendance record this year, 15,094,946, although this was undoubtedly due also to the expansion to 12 teams. And although the new rules designed to curb pitchers did indeed produce 17 .300 hitters (versus only six of them in 1968), 15 pitchers won 20 or more games – the most such in 40 years. So much for the calculations of rules committees as major league baseball prepared to embark on the 1970s.

CHAPTER SEVEN

Untraditional Seventies

. . . baseball is a business in every sense of the word. It is part of the entertainment industry.

Business Week

The 1960s are perceived as a decade of turmoil in American society in general, and to the extent that organized baseball also experienced such changes as the expansion of the numbers of teams and numerous franchise shifts, the National League also went through some turmoil of its own. But in many respects, the 1970s proved to be a more tumultuous decade for the major leagues – indeed, almost a decade of revolution. No one can ever prove these things, but to the extent that baseball is so deeply enmeshed in American society, perhaps it was no coincidence that a decade that included the collapse of the war in Vietnam and the debacle known as Watergate should also see baseball players going out on their first strike and challenging the 'reserve clause,' long regarded as the very foundation of organized baseball. After all, if American presidents traditionally throw out the baseball that opens the season and there were three different presidents in the 30 months between August 1974 and January 1977 – is it any wonder that baseball players were confused?

Quite seriously, the 1970s were in many ways distinguished by a general breakdown in respect for traditions and authority. This had begun in the 1960s in society at large, and baseball, as one of the more traditional institutions, was a bit tardy in accepting this new spirit. But when it came to baseball in the 1970s, it came in many forms. Jim Bouton's *Ball Four*, the first 'let-it-all-hang-out' book by a contemporary major leaguer, might be regarded as a signal of the change, and the players of the 1970s carried on this new spirit of rebelliousness in such ways as allowing their hair to flourish and their tempers to flare. We shall examine the challenge to and eventual defeat of the reserve clause in the proper years, but perhaps the most immediate impact on baseball's loyal fans was the sight of the newly 'liberated' players scurrying around to whichever team would pay the biggest salary.

At the same time, the 1970s can hardly be dismissed as the decade when the players went for the Big Bucks. They also went for the Big Records – and came

through: several of the most indomitable records of modern baseball would be wiped out in the 1970s – home runs, season and career stolen bases, career runs batted in, season strikeouts, season games pitched. And many fans would point out that most of these records were being re-set by National League players – a National League, furthermore, that was increasingly dominating the All-Star games and a National League that rejected the American League's adoption of arguably the most revolutionary change in modern organized baseball – the designated hitter. Purists – and these may or may not be synonymous with National League fans – might argue that any league to adopt such a device only deserved to take second place in the record books.

This decade of turmoil and change, then, was launched on 16 January 1970, when Curt Flood, a 32-year-old outfielder, filed a suit against organized baseball's so-called reserve clause. Curt Flood had played 12 years for the St Louis Cardinals and had been recognized as one of the leading players in the league; even his employer had recognized this by paying him $90,000 for the 1969 season – one of the highest salaries in both leagues. But when that season ended, Flood was traded by the Cardinals to the Philadelphia Phillies – a transaction that for decades had been taking place in organized baseball and that had been both formally enforced by the United States Supreme Court and tacitly endorsed by generations of traded players. But now here was Curt Flood charging that the reserve clause was 'a contract for perpetual service' and that he did not want to go on being treated as 'property . . . a chattel . . . a slave for a team against his will.'

What was this 'reserve clause' that could prompt such charged language? Actually, it was a series of clauses or terms that were part of the standard contract of every player in professional baseball. Under these terms, a player was legally bound to a team until he was sold or traded to another team, which in turn owned this player. Oh, a team might release a player and thus free him to sign on with another of his choice – but most players were never released until their playing days were over. And if a player didn't like a team that held him under contract, the only thing he could do was to quit professional baseball.

It does indeed sound suspiciously like a form of slavery or at the very least like a restraint of trade that had come to be struck down by American antitrust laws and rulings. Yet without ever actually ruling on the reserve clause itself, the Supreme Court, since its first landmark decision in 1922 and in several decisions in the 1950s, had held that organized baseball was not subject to the antitrust laws that governed the conduct of business in America. In fact, it was a form of tribute to baseball's special standing in American life that exempted it from such antitrust laws, for this same Supreme Court often ruled that other organized sports – hockey, boxing, professional football, for instance – did fall under the antitrust laws. Such a tribute, however, was little consolation to players who saw their salaries and movements dictated by the owners, who in turn argued that the reserve clause was the only thing that prevented the richest teams from buying all the better players – and thus upsetting the balance that allowed so many teams to remain competitive over the years.

But Curt Flood, backed by the Major League Baseball Players Association, challenged that assumption in 1970 in the United State District Court in New York

Hank Aaron crosses the plate after hitting his homer number 723 at Philadelphia, 4 June 1974. From left to right: Aaron, Darrell Evans, batboy Charlie Samuels, Ralph Garr, umpire Billy Williams, Mike Lum and the Phillies' catcher Bob Boone. Henry Louis Aaron played mainly the outfield for the Braves (1954-74) both in Milwaukee and Atlanta. He went back to Milwaukee to finish his career with the Brewers (1975-76). This Hall of Famer ended up hitting 755 home runs, a record that should last for decades if not forever, while batting .305. He led the league in hitting twice (1956 and 1959) and was named Most Valuable Player in 1957.

Above: Curt Flood, who began the fight to eliminate the reserve clause.

miracle of their 1969 triumph, but the team could not maintain that elevation. Yet on 22 April, it looked as though Tom Seaver was going to be able singlehandedly to carry the Mets to new heights: on that day, he struck out 19 batters of the San Diego Padres, thus tying Steve Carlton's record, and set a new record by striking out 10 (the last of the 19) in a row. But other Met stars of the 1969 season such as Jerry Koosman and Cleon Jones couldn't repeat, and even Seaver, although 16-5 on 1 August, fell to a 2-7 record during the closing weeks. The Mets finished third in the Eastern Division, only one game behind Chicago but six behind the division winner, Pittsburgh. The Pirates won with a re-hired manager, Danny Murtaugh, and with the help of an old standby, Roberto Clemente, who hit .353.

In the Western Division, it was almost no contest: the Reds left the second-place Dodgers 14½ games behind. They, too, had a new manager, George 'Sparky' Anderson – at 36, the youngest then in the major leagues. They also had a spectacular 22-year-old catcher, Johnny Bench, who among his other distinctions was of part Amerindian descent; not only did his sharp reflexes behind the plate give his team an edge, but his power at the plate led to 45 home runs and 148 runs batted in; both performances combined to win him the league's Most Valuable Player award. But no one player or manager wins 102 games in a season: Cincinnati blasted away the opposition with four .300 hitters: Tony Perez (.317), Pete Rose (.316), Bobby Tolan (.316), and Bernie Carbo (.306).

Cincinnati's Jim Merritt (20-12) was one of four 20-game winners in the National League; the others were Bob Gibson (23-7) of St Louis, Gaylord Perry (23-13) of San Francisco, and Ferguson Jenkins (22-16) of Chicago. No records there, but batters were assaulting all kinds of records. Hank Aaron became the 9th man in major league history to get 3000 hits, and Willy Mays was right behind him as the 10th; Ernie Banks of the Cubs became the 9th man to hit 500 home runs.

The Big Red Machine of Cincinnati went rolling along through the National League play-offs, defeating the Pirates in three straight games – although the scores (3-0 in 10 innings, 3-1, 3-2) reveal that the Pirates were hardly a pushover. But then, although the National League had won the All-Star game, 5-4 (in 12 innings), for the league's eighth straight victory, the Baltimore Orioles took Cincinnati in the World Series, 4-1. Only Lee May's three-run homer in the eighth inning of the fourth game kept the Orioles from a clean sweep.

As the 1971 season began, many picked the Cincinnati Reds to repeat in their Western Division, but their power hitters didn't produce and they finished only fourth. The division winners, instead, were the San Francisco Giants (even though they had traded George Foster to the Reds – a trade they would come to regret as the years passed). At one point, the Giants enjoyed a 10½ game lead, but as they came into the final game of the season they were leading only by one game – and that over their opponent in the game, the Los Angeles Dodgers. What had gone wrong? Well, Willie Mays, for one, was 40 and had bursitis in his shoulder, while Willie McCovey, the most powerful Giants slugger, had arthritis in his right knee and a torn cartilage in his left knee. But the Giants right fielder Bobby Bonds hit 33 home runs and in that final game the Giants came through and beat the Dodgers.

In the Eastern Division, the Pittsburgh Pirates repeated their victory, this time leaving the St Louis

City. (One of Flood's lawyers was Arthur J Goldberg, a former associate justice of the Supreme Court.) The District Court soon ruled that it could not overturn the decisions of the Supreme Court regarding baseball; Flood appealed this decision to the US Circuit Court of Appeals, which upheld the District Court; Flood then appealed to the Supreme Court itself. It would be 1972 before the Supreme Court ruled that since baseball remained exempt from antitrust laws, the reserve clause was legal; however, the majority opinion went on to call this exemption an 'aberration' and called on Congress to reconsider the special status accorded organized baseball – since even its most devoted fans could hardly deny that it had become a business. (Whether it was Big or Show would be a question that would emerge in the late 70s and early 80s.)

Curt Flood, meanwhile, sat out the 1970 season – a considerable sacrifice for a player at his salary level. In November of that year, however, assured that it would not prejudice his suit still being appealed, he signed with the Washington Senators when they acquired his contract in a trade with the Phillies. (Yes, it included the reserve clause.)

When the season began, the New York Mets and all their fans were still euphoric over the incredible

Above: Roberto Clemente scores while playing for Los Cangrejeros in the Puerto Rican Winter League.

Cardinals seven games behind. The Pirates may not have had any superstars, but they had a team of solid players such as Al Oliver, Dave Cash, Rob Robertson, and Manny Sanguillen (who would go on to become a great catcher); they had Willie Stargell who got hot and hit 48 home runs to lead the league (and the majors); and in Roberto Clemente, in right field and hitting .341, they had a player who was on the verge of finally being recognized as one of the game's best all-round players.

Certainly the Pirates did not win on pitching. The pitching stars of 1971 played elsewhere. Tom Seaver of the Mets not only had a record of 20-10 but the lowest earned-run average in the majors – 1.76. Meanwhile, Ferguson Jenkins (24-13) pitched his fifth consecutive 20-game season and also racked up the astonishing stat of only 37 walks in 327 innings. Hank Aaron hit 47 home runs and raised his total to 639 – a career high trailing only Willie Mays' 646 and Ruth's seemingly impregnable 714. But with Aaron still going strong, that 714 no longer looked quite so remote.

In the National League play-offs, the Giants beat the Pirates in the first game, 5-4, but led by Bob Robertson's four home runs, the Pirates swept the next three, 9-4, 2-1, 9-5. Even so, the Pirates went into the World Series against the Orioles as the underdogs. After all, hadn't Baltimore wiped out the Big Red Machine in the 1970 series, won the last 11 games of

their regular season, and then taken the Oakland A's in three straight? And when the Series opened in Baltimore and the Orioles took the first two games, 5-3 and 11-3, even the most loyal Pirates fans must have had a sinking feeling. But then the Pirates mounted a boarding party – and behind the superb pitching of Steve Blass, Bruce Kison and Nelson Briles, and the strong hitting of Roberto Clemente, Pittsburgh took the next three, 5-1, 4-3, and 4-0. The fourth game, incidentally, was the first night game in the history of the World Series.

Back in Baltimore, the Orioles took the sixth game, 3-2, but only on Brooks Robinson's sacrifice fly in the 10th inning. And then, in one of those cliffhangers that give the World Series such a special role in Americans' memories, Steve Blass held the Orioles to four hits and the Pirates took the final game, 2-1, and became the World Champions. Once again, it was a team effort, but the whole country now had had a chance to see just what a consummate player Clemente was: he hit .414 in the series, his 12 hits falling just one short of the record in a Series but like his fielding, coming exactly where and when needed to keep his team ahead.

The 1972 season began somewhat inauspiciously during the training-exhibition weeks as the players in both major leagues were demanding that the club owners contribute more to the medical and pension

Above: Joe Morgan takes a cut. Joseph Leonard Morgan has played with several teams during his career, which began in Houston in 1963. He won back-to-back Most Valuable Player Awards in 1975 and 1976, when he was with the Cincinnati Reds.
Opposite: Steve Carlton lets one go. Stephen Norman 'Lefty' Carlton pitched for the Cardinals and the Phillies. His ERA is usually around 3.00 and in 1972 he struck out 310 batters. He won the Cy Young Award in 1972, 1977 and 1980.

funds. Finally the players went out on a strike for 10 days – the first general strike in the history of organized baseball. The strike ended on 13 April, but 86 regular season games had been missed; it was decided not to try to make them up, so various teams in the majors ended up playing different numbers of games. It was only one of many indications that the traditional immutability of major league baseball was beginning to bend to the realities of modern life. Imagine the players of 50 years earlier striking for medical benefits and salaries of over $100,000 a year. And although the Supreme Court ruled this same spring that the reserve clause was legal and that Curt Flood's contract still held, there were portents of the future in the Court's urging of Congress to reconsider baseball's exemption from antitrust legislation.

But once on the field, the players gave the fans another exciting season. In the Eastern Division, the Pirates won for the third consecutive year, leaving the Cubs 11 games behind in second place. The Pirates succeeded with a combination of hitting and pitching, and once again Clemente came through, hitting .312 for the season; on the last day of the season, he got his 3000th hit, the 11th player in the history of baseball till then to achieve this. In the Western Division,

Cincinnati's Big Red Machine – powered by Johnny Bench's 40 home runs and 125 runs batted in – took first place, leaving Houston 10½ games behind. The talk of the season, though, was Manager Sparky Anderson's habit of quickly removing his pitchers as soon as they got into a bit of trouble: only 25 Cincinnati pitchers survived complete games, while Sparky gained a new nickname, 'Captain Hook.' The Reds then went on to beat the Pirates in the league play-offs, but it took them all five games and a wild pitch by the Pirates Bob Moose in the bottom of the ninth inning of the final game.

The World Series pitted the Reds against the Oakland A's and it went into seven games before Oakland won that, 3-2, and became the champions. Except for the A's' Gene Tenace's four homers, equaling a record shared by Babe Ruth and Lou Gehrig, the series was dominated by the pitchers: the Reds' combined batting performance was held to .208, the A's to .207 and six of the seven games were decided by one run (a record). But the most spectacular pitching of the entire season was that of Steve Carlton, who had been traded away by the Cardinals to the Phillies; while posting a 27-10 record, he completed 30 of 41 starts, struck out 310, and ended with an earned run average

on those terms by the National League – here, as so often, the somewhat more conservative of the leagues. (Although it might be pointed out that it would be National League players who would take the lead in setting aside the reserve clause. . . .) In the immediate sense, the designated hitter rule did what its proponents promised: the American League scored more runs and raised its over-all batting average (and it also saw the American League setting a new attendance record for the league). So successful was it, in fact, that the American League adopted the designated hitter permanently at the end of the 1973 season. (And it was agreed that World Series would be played with the designated hitter allowed only in alternate years.)

The 'miracle' of the 1973 season was a re-run of the 1969 season by the Mets. On 30 August, the Mets were in last place in the Eastern Division. Then, fired up by their star relief pitcher, Tug McGraw, with his cry of 'Ya gotta believe!' the Mets won 20 of their last 28 games and came rolling into the last day of the season needing to win at least one game of a doubleheader against Chicago to keep St Louis and Pittsburgh from tying with them for first place. The Mets took the first game – taking their division lead with a win-lost percentage of only .509 (the lowest of any pennant winner in baseball history). In fact, the Mets had been outscored by every team they played except one and their team batting average of .246 left them in 9th place in the National League. The Mets best pitcher was Tom Seaver, but his record was only 19-10 (and the Mets had traded another young pitcher, Nolan Ryan, to the California Angels – where his 383 strikeouts broke by one the modern major-league record that Sandy Koufax set in 1965).

In the Western Division, the Cincinnati Reds made their own fairly spectacular 'charge': at one point 11 games behind the Dodgers, they overtook them and then left them 3½ games in second place. Led by Pete Rose (.338, 230 hits), Tony Perez (.314, 27 homers), Joe Morgan (.290, 26 homers) and Johnny Bench (25 homers), the Big Red Machine once again seemed invincible. But in the National League play-offs, the

Above: Tug McGraw after he was traded by the New York Mets to the Philadelphia Phillies.

of only 1.98. And all this for a team that finished in last place.

A year that began with the death of the Mets manager, Gil Hodges, in spring training, and then saw the death of Hodges' old Brooklyn teammate, Jackie Robinson – always to be respected for pioneering the way for black players in the major leagues – ended on a truly tragic note. Roberto Clemente was in Puerto Rico, his homeland, when an earthquake devastated Managua, Nicaragua; on 31 December, he joined others on a DC-7 that was to fly supplies from San Juan to the earthquake victims; barely airborne, the plane crashed into the sea, taking Clemente to his death. Among the bitter ironies was that Clemente had never liked all the flying that went with modern major league schedules; and a player who had often gone unrecognized in his long career was given the ultimate recognition when the Hall of Fame waived its traditional five-year rule in 1973 and voted him immediately into baseball's shrine.

The 1973 season seemed to be one of those that come along every few years – a season full of oddities. It began with one of the most revolutionary changes in the basic rules of baseball since the modern game was organized: the adoption of the designated hitter by the American League. Although announced as merely a three-year experiment, it was rejected even

Far right: Tony Perez. Atanasio Rigal Perez began his career with the Reds in 1964, then went to Montreal in 1977.

Mets caught them off-guard and behind the pitching of Seaver, Koosman and Matlack, the Mets beat the Reds in five games. One of the less admirable episodes in the season came in the third game when both teams rushed onto the field after Pete Rose of the Reds got into a fight with Bud Harrelson of the Mets – and then the Mets fans threw so many objects at Rose that Sparky Anderson refused to continue playing until manager Yogi Berra and some of his players went out and calmed down their fans.

The Mets' dream of repeating their 1969 miracle, however, was not to be, as the Oakland A's defeated them, 4 games to 3. But the World Series this year was somewhat overshadowed by Hank Aaron's pursuit of Babe Ruth's career record of 714 homeruns: when the season ended, Aaron had hit 40, bringing his total to 713. (His fellow Braves, Darrell Evans and Dave Johnson had hit 41 and 43, respectively – the first time that any major league club could boast of three 40-homer men in a season.) It was obvious that Ruth's record was going to fall in 1974.

So obvious, in fact, that when the 1974 season began, the owners of the Atlanta Braves decided they would order Aaron to sit out the first three games, which the Braves were scheduled to play in Cincinnati, so that Aaron would most likely break the record at his home field. An understandable desire, but Bowie Kuhn, commissioner of baseball, overruled

Pete Rose playing third base.

the Braves. And so it was that when Hank Aaron came to bat for the first time in the opening game on 4 April, on his first swing he hit his 714th home run. Then, on 8 April, playing before 53,000 in the Atlanta stadium (and a television audience estimated at 35,000,000) Aaron hit the record-breaking 715th home run (off the Dodgers' Al Downing). Aaron had come in for an incredible amount of pressure – and abuse – for taking over Babe Ruth's record, but he himself was gracious after his moment of triumph: 'It's the Cadillac of baseball records. But Babe Ruth will still be regarded as the greatest home run hitter who ever lived.' That may be true for a certain generation, but the recordbooks will long show that Henry Aaron has hit the most home runs.

The 1974 season was distinguished by two other new records. One still stands: Mike Marshall, who only the year before, while pitching for Montreal, had appeared in 92 games, set a new record by appearing in 106 games for the Los Angeles Dodgers. The other record would eventually be broken, but at the time it seemed monumental: Lou Brock of the Cardinals

broke Maury Wills 1962 record of 104 stolen bases in a season by stealing 118. On the one hand, it was not a surprise, as Brock had led the National League in stolen bases for seven of the last eight years; what was amazing was that Brock was 35 and seemed to have reached his peak during the 1960s as a power hitter.

The regular season of 1974 provided no special excitement. In the Eastern Division, the Pirates managed to squeeze by St Louis by 1½ games, mostly due to the heavy hitting of Richie Hebner, Willie Stargell, Al Oliver and Richie Zisk. (The Pirates' best pitcher, Jerry Reuss, only had 16 wins.) In the Western Division, the Dodgers led from the first week, and ended up four games ahead of the Reds. Along with Andy Messersmith's 20 wins – and Mike Marshall's 106 appearances at the mound – the Dodgers could count on a superbly coordinated infield: Steve Garvey at first, Davey Lopes at second, Bill Russell at shortstop and Ron Cey at third – they would play together through 1981. In the National League playoffs, the Dodgers took the Pirates in four games, with Don Sutton winning two of these by holding the Pirates to

Below: Lou Brock of the St Louis Cardinals breaks for second in an attempted steal against the Pittsburgh Pirates.

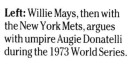 **Left:** Willie Mays, then with the New York Mets, argues with umpire Augie Donatelli during the 1973 World Series.

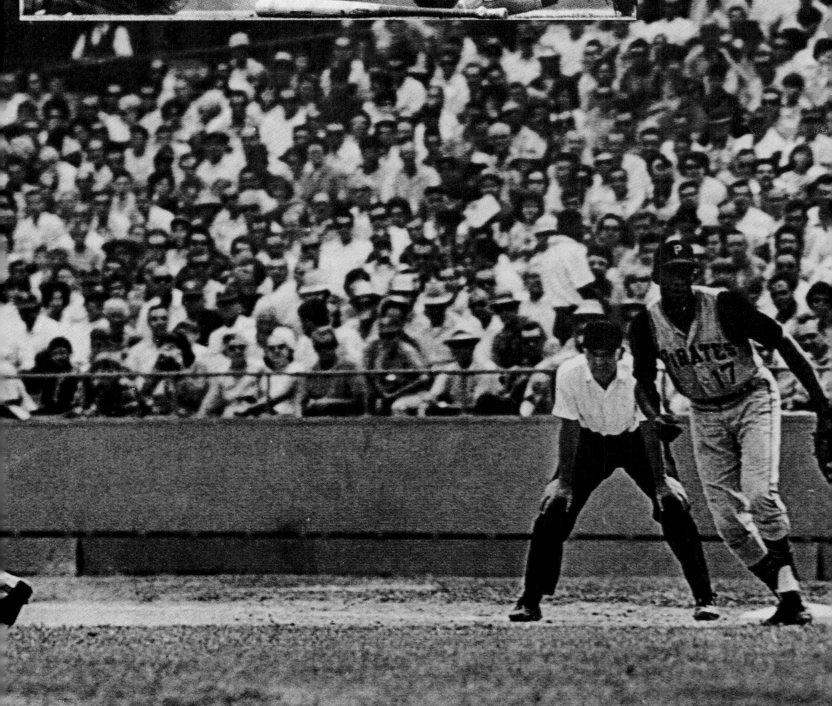

Above: Mike Marshall delivers one to the plate. Michael Grant Marshall, a relief pitcher for the Tigers, the Astros, the Expos, the Dodgers, the Braves, the Rangers and the Twins, began his career in 1967. He won the Cy Young Award in 1974 while he was with the Dodgers.
Right: Dave McNally on the mound. David Arthur McNally pitched for the Baltimore Orioles (1962-74) and the Montreal Expos (1975), winning 184 games and losing 119 with a 3.24 earned run average.

seven hits. In the World Series, however, the Dodgers lost out to the Oakland A's, four games to one – despite the A's strange uniforms, moustaches, and antics: as Dodgers Manager Walt Alston put it, 'They play the game the way it should be played.'

The 1975 baseball season is memorable primarily for its post-season activities – both on and off the playing field. For the regular season produced few surprises. In the Eastern Division, the Pittsburgh Pirates took their fifth title in six years, leaving the Phillies 6½ games behind. And in the Western Division, the Cincinnati Reds won 108 games – the third highest total ever, and the best record since Pittsburgh won 110 in 1909 – and left the Dodgers 20 games behind in second place. They achieved this awesome feat with some heavy hitting and by Manager Sparky Anderson's clever – and frequent – use of relief pitchers (none of his pitchers won over 15

games). The Big Red Machine then went rolling over the Pirates in the playoffs in three straight games.

Considering that the American League champions were the Boston Red Sox, who surprised everyone by beating out the Oakland A's, the Reds looked like a shoe-in for the Series. True, Boston had a hot young rookie, Fred Lynn – their other hot rookie, Jim Rice, missed the last of the season due to a broken hand – but even Boston's Lynn and Yastrzemski seemed out-classed by the Reds' Joe Morgan, Pete Rose, Johnny Bench and Tony Perez. Yet the Red Sox took the Reds to the seventh game, which the Reds won in the 9th inning on Morgan's single. The sixth game had taken over four hours to play, going into 12 innings and ending at 12:33 AM. And the third game provided one of those incidents that true fans would always argue over: Ed Armbrister of the Reds bunted in the 10th inning, and then failed to move away fast enough, so

that Fisk, the Sox catcher, bumped into him; Fisk's resultant bad throw allowed a Red to get to third and Armbrister to get to second; the Reds then scored and won 6-5.

But even this controversy was overshadowed by what happened on 23 December 1975. Andy Messer-smith of the Los Angeles Dodgers and Dave McNally of the Montreal Expos had chosen to play the 1975 season without signing contracts – and they argued that therefore they were now 'free agents,' able to sign with any team they chose to negotiate with. The owners naturally disputed this, for it effectively did away with the reserve clause. It was essentially a re-run of Curt Flood's challenge of 1970, but this time the players tried an end run – not treating it as a fundamental legal issue but merely a contractual dis-pute. So the issue went not into the courts but into arbitration, and in December the arbitrator, Peter M

Steve Garvey at first base. Steve Patrick Garvey played primarily first base for the Los Angeles Dodgers, beginning in 1969. He was later traded to the San Diego Padres. He usually bats around .300 and was the National League Player of the Year in 1974.

Right: Andy Messersmith. John Alexander Messersmith pitched in both the National and the American Leagues, beginning with the Angels in 1968. His earned run average was usually below 3.00.

Seitz, ruled that Messersmith and McNally were indeed free agents – that a player's contract cannot be renewed indefinitely by the original owner until the player is traded, sold, released or retires.

Thus in one neat blow was organized baseball's hallowed keystone, the reserve clause, struck down. Not immediately, though, for the owners contended that the arbitrator's ruling was limited to only Messersmith and McNally. The owners then decided to have the decision set aside by the courts, after all, and since there was no resolution of the dispute by 1 March 1976, when spring training was to begin, the owners simply refused to open the camps. On 17 March, though, when there were signs of compromise, Commissioner Bowie Kuhn ordered that spring training begin immediately. And on the eve of the All-Star Game, 12 July, the players and owners finally announced they had agreed on a new basic contract. After five years in the major leagues, a player could demand to be traded; if he was not, he could become a free agent. Then, after six years in the majors, a player could become a free agent; however,

he could negotiate only with a maximum of 13 clubs (including his present one) that had acquired the right to bargain in this re-entry draft.

At once the cry went up – and not only from the owners themselves – that this would be the end of true competition within the major leagues: the few very rich owners and clubs would always be able to buy up the best free agents and the teams would be divided among 'the haves and the have-nots.' And at first it did appear this way. Andy Messersmith, fittingly enough, seems to have become the first major league 'millionaire' now that he was free to leave the Dodgers and sign with the Atlanta Braves in April 1976. And when the first free-agent draft was held on 4 November 1976, numerous players did sign contracts for large sums of money. But it did not lead immediately to any drastic split between the richer and the poorer clubs, nor could anyone prove that a roster of millionaires guaranteed a pennant. There would always be the unpredictable element in baseball – the rookies who came out of nowhere to spark a team, the 'over-the-hill' veterans who produced some grand

final efforts, and above all the inexplicable team spirit – perhaps best shown by the Mets of 1969 – that defied all the bookmakers and bookkeepers.

The 1976 season itself produced no particular surprises. Once again the Cincinnati Reds swept the Western Division, winning 102 games and leaving the Dodgers 10 games behind; with a team batting average of .280, the highest in the majors, five of their eight regulars batted over .300; the Reds also led defensively, with the highest fielding percentage and the fewest errors. In the Eastern Division, the Phillies beat out Pittsburgh, but even with Mike Schmidt, Greg Luzinski, Garry Maddox and 20-game winner Steve Carlton, the Phillies fell in three straight to the Reds in the playoffs. There was no stopping the Big Red Machine after that, and they wiped out the Yankees four straight in the World Series, thus becoming the first National League team to repeat as World Champions since the New York Giants had done so in 1922.

The 1976 season, in fact, was memorable less for what happened on the field than what occurred around the negotiating table. But for the National League, it was also memorable for the retirement of two of its longtime stars. Walter Alston, after 23 years as manager of the Dodgers, retired. And Henry Aaron, also winding up his 23rd year as a major leaguer, retired at age 42; his 755 home runs now stood as a record that seemed unassailable as Ruth's 714 once did, while Aaron's 3771 lifetime hits at the time left him second only to Ty Cobb. It was hard not to think of it as the end of an era.

Above: Mike Schmidt takes a cut. Michael Jack Schmidt has played third base for the Philadelphia Phillies since he broke into baseball in 1972. A prodigious long-ball hitter, he won back-to-back Most Valuable Player Awards in 1980 and 1981.

Far left: Tony Perez (#24) about to shake Pete Rose's hand after Rose scored a game-winning run for the Reds against the Phillies.

But if Alston was gone from the Dodgers, the Dodgers were not gone from the National League. In 1977, they came charging back under their rookie manager, Tom Lasorda, and won the Western Division, leaving the Reds the same 10 games behind that the Dodgers had been in 1976. Both teams seemed loaded with talent, in fact. The Dodgers had a 20-game winner in Tommy John, while four of their players – Garvey, Ron Cey, Reggie Smith and Dusty Baker – hit 30 or more homers. Meantime, the Reds had Tom Seaver (who had asked to be traded from the Mets because of a contract dispute) and a one-man power-house in George Foster, who hit 25 home runs and batted in 149 runs. (Voted the league's Most Valuable Player, he was the fifth Red in the last six years to be so honored.)

In the Eastern Division, the Chicago Cubs led in the early part of the season, but they faded and the Phillies won the title again, with Pittsburgh five games behind. Steve Carlton came through with a 23-10 season, while Mike Schmidt hit 40 homers and Greg Luzinski hit 39. In the pennant playoffs, however, the Phillies fell to the Dodgers in four games. In the Series, the Dodgers in turn fell to the Yankees, four games to

Tommy LaSorda, the Dodger manager. Thomas Charles LaSorda pitched for just three years in the majors – for Brooklyn (1954-55) and Kansas City (1956) – winning no games and losing four with his 6.48 earned run average. But it was as a manager that his genius became evident. Beginning the job in Los Angeles in 1976, he has won five Western Division Championships, three National League pennants and one World Series.

Right: George Foster at the plate. George Arthur Foster, whose career in the outfield began in San Francisco in 1969, has played with Cincinnati and New York in the National League. He twice was the league's home run leader (1977 and 1978, while at Cincinnati) and in 1977 was the Most Valuable Player in the National League.
Opposite: Tom Seaver when he played for the Cincinnati Reds.

two – or perhaps it would be more exact to say the Dodgers fell to Reggie Jackson, who set records of five home runs and 10 runs scored for a Series, three successive home runs and four runs scored in a single game.

But an even more fundamental record of major league baseball fell in 1977, when on 29 August Lou Brock of the St Louis Cardinals stole his 893rd base, breaking Ty Cobb's lifetime record of 892. Attendance records were being set, too, as Los Angeles set an all-time major league record for one club, with 2,900,000 fans at its 79 home games. And the 26 major league teams – the American League had added two more teams this year – boasted 38,700,000 spectators, a 24 percent increase over 1976, the previous record year. Any fear that the 'desertions' by free agents in pursuit of the Top Dollar might turn off the fans was proving groundless.

The 1978 season seemed in many ways a re-run of the 1977 season. In the Western Division of the

Below: Lou Brock of the St Louis Cardinals avoids the tag at home.

National League, the Dodgers beat out the Reds again, but only after the Reds collapsed after 6 August, losing 15 of their next 21 games, and the Dodgers went on to win 22 of their last 37 games. The Dodgers achieved their victory without any particular superstars – only Steve Garvey took a lead in statistics, with his 202 hits – but some good pitching by Tommy John, Burt Hooton and Don Sutton, plus Tom Lasorda's savvy managing did the trick. In the Eastern Division, the Phillies and Pittsburgh battled it out again, with the Phillies taking their third consecutive title in the division. In the playoffs, the Dodgers were leading two games to one, when in the tenth inning of the fourth game, the Phillies Garry Maddox, usually the most surehanded of players, dropped a flyball and the Dodgers took the game and that series.

The Dodgers went into the World Series against the Yankees again, but this time they were favored – in part because the Yankees were coming out of a sea-

son in which good playing was overshadowed by bad conduct. When the Dodgers took the first two games, it appeared that the Good Guys would win – but then the Yankees went on to take the next four and become the first team ever to lose the first two of the World Series and come back to win it in six. All Ron Cey of the Dodgers could say was, 'They had better pitching, defense and hitting. What else is there?'

1978 was the year, though, that one of the National League's long favorite players began to claim everyone's serious attention. On 14 June, Pete Rose of the Reds began a hitting streak that first broke the modern National League record of 37, by Tommy Holmes in 1945, and then went on to hit safely in 44 games, tying the all-time National League record set by Wee Willie Keeler in 1897. And on 5 May, Rose had become the 13th player in major-league history to get 3000 hits in a career. At the end of the season, though, Rose surprised everyone, and disappointed some of his special Cincinnati fans, by signing a four-year contract (for $3,200,000) with the Phillies. The Reds had already fired their manager, Sparky Anderson, and it looked as though the Cincinnati dynasty had come to an end.

But the Reds held in there for the 1979 season, and with solid performances by George Foster, Johnny Bench, Dave Concepcion and Tom Seaver, they led the Western Division, with Houston 1½ games behind. Meanwhile, over in the Eastern Division, the Phillies – despite Rose's .331 batting average and his tenth season with over 200 hits – could only come in fourth. The winner in the East was Pittsburgh, and it was confirmation that team effort still counted at least as much as astronomical salaries, as welcome as they might be for the individual recipients. Willie Stargell, now 39 and fondly known as 'Pops,' came up with 32 home runs (and won himself a tie for the Most Valuable Player, with Keith Hernandez of St Louis); Omar Moreno stole 77 bases and Kent Tekulve, Enrique Romo and Grant Jackson appeared as relief pitchers in a total of 250 games. The Pirates then went on to defeat the Reds in the league playoffs in three straight games.

The World Series was a fitting climax to the decade of extremes and upsets. For one thing, many of the games were played in the rain and cold, with players' fingers really numb on occasion. The Orioles represented the American League and soon moved into the lead with three games to one for the Pirates. But in the last three games, the Pirates held the Orioles to only 17 hits and two runs; Stargell was the inspiration, making four hits, including two home runs, in the last game. The Pirates had done the near-impossible (for in fact, three other teams had previously done it) winning the World Series after being down three games to one.

Several individual National League players stood out in 1979. Lou Brock of the Cardinals got his 3000th hit, the 14th player in major league history to do so. J Rodney Richards of the Houston Astros struck out 313, a new league record for righthanders. And in one of the most unusual situations, two brothers – Phil Niekro (21-20) of the Atlanta Braves and Joe Niekro (21-11) of the Houston Astros – led the National League in victories. And with a new all-time regular season attendance record of 43,548,450 (eight teams bettered 2,000,000 at home), it seemed that major league baseball, for all the vicissitudes of the 1970s, was in a strong position to take on the challenging decade of the 1980s.

Opposite: Some of the 'Bleacher Bums' in the friendly confines of Wrigley Field in Chicago – the oldest ball park in the National League – which boasts no lights and natural grass.

Below: The Pittsburgh Pirates leave the dugout to hug Willie Stargell after he scores against the Baltimore Orioles in the 1979 World Series.

CHAPTER EIGHT

The Decade Past and Present

The game gave me a great feeling.

Pete Rose on the Opening Day game, 1985

It would take several decades before major league baseball of the 1980s could be seen in true perspective. But if other decades might be characterized as those of the Big Bats or the Big Strikeouts, then viewed close up, the 1980s seemed to be the decade of the Big Bucks and the Big Strikes. The era of the Big Bucks, of course, really began with the effective discarding of the reserve clause in 1976 and the resultant boom in the free-agent market. Between 1978 and 1981, for instance, 43 players received contracts worth over a million dollars to each; the then summit was attained by Dave Winfield in November 1980 when he signed a ten-year contract with the New York Yankees worth a reported $13,000,000 (with a cost-of-living clause that could make it worth at least $20,000,000). And not only were the free agents and superstars of the game enjoying this boom; all players were riding the wave, as the average salary of all major-league players advanced from $50,000 in 1976 to $200,000 in 1981.

The Big Strike followed directly in the wake of the Big Bucks, because the owners decided in 1980 that they would try to gain some adantage from the free-agent boom. The owners demanded that any club that lost a player because of the free agent move must get a player from the club that signed the free agent. The players, through their formal Players' Association, naturally objected; they staged a walkout during the final week of spring training and threatened to go on strike on 23 May 1980 if there was no agreement with the owners; minutes before the deadline, the club owners and the Players' Association agreed to set up a player-management committee to study the issue of free agency and proper payment; if agreement was not reached by 31 January 1981, each side in the dispute could take whatever action it was prepared to support.

So the disagreement was temporarily sidetracked and the 1980 season proceeded. And proceed it did right up to the last day – plus one, for the Western

Below: Cesar Cedeño at bat as a Houston Astro. He later went to the Reds and then the Cardinals.

Division of the National League. This was the year that another so-called expansion team made its challenge against a tough veteran team – the Houston Astros, that is, in existence only since 1962, found itself fighting for the division lead against the Los Angeles Dodgers. Houston had lost out in 1979 by only 1½ games to Cincinnati, and they still had a couple of ace pitchers in Joe Niekro and J R Richard, but Richard suffered a stroke in July. Still, going into their last three games, the Astros had a three-game lead – except that their opponent in these last games was the Los Angeles Dodgers. The Dodgers took all three, so there had to be a single game playoff to determine the division winner. Joe Niekro won it for the Astros, who then had to face the Eastern Division winner, the Philadelphia Phillies. The Phillies were loaded with talent – having acquired Pete Rose in 1979, and with Mike Schmidt hitting 48 home runs and Steve Carlton winning 24 games – but even so they did not tie up the Eastern Division title until the next-to-last game of the season, and then only beating off Montreal with Schmidt's home run. .

The National League playoff for the pennant proved to be one of the most exciting and exacting in recent memory. It went into the fifth game – with four games going into extra innings – but experience finally provided the edge and the Phillies took the fifth game. It was only the third time in their long history that the Phillies had made it into a World Series, and in their first, in 1915, they had lost to the Red Sox, four games to one, while in 1950 they had been swept away in four straight games by the Yankees. But 1980 proved to be the Phillies' year. They met the Kansas City Royals and defeated them four games to two. Mike Schmidt was voted the Most Valuable Player of the Series, with his .381 batting average, two of the Phillies' three homers, and team-leading seven runs batted in.

One of the most memorable games of the 1980 season was that pitched by Jerry Reuss of the Los Angeles Dodgers against the San Francisco Giants, on 28 June. In the first inning, Dodger shortstop Bill Russell made a slight throwing error and Jack Clark got to first base. But he was the only Giant to get to first base: Reuss then retired the next 25 batters in a row and thus missed a perfect game by that one error.

The 1981 season began under a cloud, for the Players' Association and the owners had still not resolved their differences over the issues of free agents. The owners had come up with what they regarded as a compromise: for every 'premium' player who left a club as a free agent, that club was to be given a professional replacement by the club that

Left: Mike Schmidt at third base for the Philadelphia Phillies. Schmidt led the league in home runs seven times – 1974, 1975, 1976, 1980, 1982, 1983 and 1984 and was the runs batted in leader in 1980, 1981, and 1984.

Opposite: Steve Garvey avoids catcher Ed Ott's tag in a game between the Dodgers and the Pirates.

Above: Tim Raines of the Montreal Expos at bat. Raines is a consistent .300 hitter.

Far right: Determination shows on the face of Dodger pitcher Fernando Valenzuela. Valenzuela won the Cy Young Award in 1981 as well as the Rookie of the Year Award that same year.

signed the free agent. A 'premium player' was to be so designated by a complicated formula involving his statistics in relation to other players of his position. The players saw this as still restricting the negotiating rights of players and although they began the season they made it clear that they were prepared to strike.

But this did not stop the players from giving their best as the season commenced. There were close races going in all four divisions of the major leagues, attendance was setting new records and there were a couple of sensational rookies in Tim Raines of the Montreal Expos and Fernando Valenzuela of the Dodgers. Valenzuela, in fact, became a national celebrity. Only 20 years old and from Mexico – he spoke very little English – he had pitched in relief in 1980 but now this lefthander was literally unbeatable: by 14 May he had an 8-0 record, five of those shutouts. Baseball was the talk of the nation.

And then suddenly there was no baseball to talk about: on 12 June, exactly as they had warned they might, the players went on strike. It went on for 50 days – the longest strike in the history of organized sports – and before it ended and play resumed, 714 games were cancelled. The terms of the settlement, which were agreed to on 31 July, were fairly com-

plicated, but they represented a compromise: teams losing 'premium' free agents would receive compensation from a pool of players that drew on all clubs rather than just from the signing club, and the teams that lost players through the pool would be compensated from a fund maintained by all the clubs. In effect, by dispersing the cost and impact, the owners would be more inclined to compete for the free agents.

That took care of the legal technicalities – but what about the game and its fans? Some people were so disgusted at what they regarded as a violation of a sacred rite that they vowed never to attend another

Below: Steve Rogers on the mound for the Montreal Expos. Stephen Douglas Rogers has had an earned run average of about 3.00 since coming to the Expos in 1973.

major league game. Others simply turned to minor league games. (In the end, everyone seems to have returned to the fold.) But in an attempt to introduce a new race into the split season, the club owners got Commissioner Bowie Kuhn to establish a 'second season.' The four teams leading their divisions when the strike began would meet their respective division winners from the second half. Everyone had alternative plans or objections to this one, but one obvious flaw was the possibility that a team might have the best total record for the year but still not have led in either half (the two halves not actually involving the same number of games).

And that is exactly what happened. In the Western Division, the Cincinnati Reds had the best total record, 62 wins and 42 losses, but it came in second – by only ½ game! – to the Dodgers in the first part of the season; then in the second part of the season, the Reds were beaten out by the Houston Astros. And in the Eastern Division, the St Louis Cardinals also had the best over-all record – 59 wins and 43 losses – but the Phillies beat them out in the first half and the Expos took the second half – again, with the Cardinals only ½ game out.

Then began what seemed like an endless series of playoffs. The Dodgers beat the Houston Astros three games to two, but only after losing the first two; the Expos defeated the Phillies also three games to two, but they did it the other way – winning the first two, dropping the next two, and then taking the fifth. Then came the playoff for the league pennant, and most people once again picked the experienced Dodgers to eliminate the young expansion team, the Expos. They did, but it took five hard games to do so. Valenzuela lost the second game and Jerry Reuss lost the third game, so the Dodgers needed to win the last two. They evened the series in a 7-1 win with Burt Hooton giving up only five hits in 7½ innings. The fifth game was rained out but rescheduled for the next day. Ray Burris pitched for the Expos and Valenzuela pitched for the Dodgers, and going into the ninth inning it was a 1-1 tie. By then, Steve Rogers had relieved Burris, and with two out he threw a sinker that Rick Monday hit over the centerfield fence; the Dodgers held off the Expos and won the game and pennant, 2-1.

The Dodgers then went on to meet the New York Yankees for the 11th time in a World Series – the Yankees having won eight of the previous. And when the Yankees took the first two games, it looked like they were going to continue their dominance. Only one other team in Series history had come back to take the next four – and that team had been the Yankees, when they did so against the Dodgers in 1978. But this year was to be different, as the Dodgers took the next four games, winning their first Series since 1965. It was a true team effort, too, so that for the first time in Series history three players shared the most valuable player award – the Dodgers' Ron Cey, Steve Yeager and Pedro Guerrero.

The 1981 season, although overwhelmed by the Big Strike, did in fact witness several records in the National League. Nolan Ryan, pitching for the Astros against the Dodgers on 26 September, got his fifth career no-hitter, a major league record (he had been sharing the record of four with Sandy Koufax). Tom Seaver of the Cincinnati Reds got his 3000th strikeout in a game against the Cardinals on 18 April and took over fifth place on the all-time strikeout list; then on 29 April, Steve Carlton got his 3000th strikeout in a game against the Montreal Expos, and he took over sixth place on the all-time list. Both Seaver and Carlton would continue their climb up the list in the years that followed.

Another National League player who was making his own assault on the record books was Pete Rose, and on 10 August 1981 he got his 3361st hit, thus moving ahead of Stan Musial's National League record – set in 1963, in a game where Rose had been present. Rose got his record-breaking hit against these same Cardinals, and was now free to take on the all-time major league record of total hits, Ty Cobb's 4191.

The 1982 season might be characterized as the roller-coaster season for the two principal headliners of major league baseball that year – Bowie Kuhn and the Atlanta Braves. For Bowie Kuhn, after 14 years as Commissioner of Baseball, it was out-again, in-again, as some of the owners organized a move to oust him; they finally succeeded in November (although even then he was asked to stay on until a successor could be chosen). It was primarily National League club owners, spearheaded by Nelson Doubleday, principal owner of the New York Mets, who opposed Kuhn on a mixture of personal style and economic motives.

In some respects the Atlanta Braves came out of 1982 no better than Bowie Kuhn. They started off the season in April with an incredible 13 straight wins –

Above: Pete Rose while he played for the Montreal Expos.
Left: Nolan Ryan pitching for the Houston Astros.

setting a new National League record – not losing their first game until the Reds defeated them on 22 April. By the end of July, the Braves seemed uncatchable: the Padres were nine games behind, the Dodgers 10. But then in August the Braves went into a tailspin and the Dodgers and Giants came alive. Because the Dodgers beat the Braves in two series in August, by the end of the month Los Angeles had taken over first place.

How had it happened? It was one of those mysteries that make baseball continually exciting. There was no single factor. Fernando Valenzuela, who had begun the season by threatening to sit it out because of a contract dispute, ended up getting the pay he felt he deserved and then was having a less than spectacular season. True, the Dodgers had Steve Garvey, 'Mr. Clean,' who became only the fifth major leaguer to play in 1000 consecutive games. But the Braves had Dale Murphy – eventually named Most Valuable Player of the league – and hard-hitting Bob Horner. In any case, when the final weekend of the season came around, the Braves had managed to sneak back into first place, but only by one game over the Dodgers and the Giants; in one of those flukes of scheduling, the Dodgers and Giants were to play a three-game series at the end, so one of them was clearly going to be knocked out of the running. The Dodgers beat the Giants in the first two, so the Giants were out. Meanwhile, the Braves were facing the Padres that last weekend in a three-game series, and the Braves also took their first two. This meant that on the last day, the Braves needed either a win or a Dodgers loss to clinch the Western Division. The Braves lost to the Padres, but Joe Morgan of the Giants hit a three-run homer to lead his team over the Dodgers. So the Braves that had seemed unbeatable in April just sneaked into first place in October.

In the Eastern Division there was a less dramatic race. The Reds, usually a major threat, were having a poor season, as were the Pirates; each team had a once-great star who was in decline – Tom Seaver for the Reds, Willie Stargell for the Pirates. (Stargell, in fact, announced that this was his last season, come what may.) But Montreal seemed strong, with the likes of Al Oliver, Gary Carter and Andre Dawson. And the Phillies were back in there, with two veterans leading the way: Pete Rose was still hitting, getting his 3771st hit on 21 June and thus tying Hank Aaron's record for second place in the majors; and Steve Carlton was to be the only 20-game winner in the

Opposite: Dale Murphy of the Atlanta Braves. Dale Bryan Murphy broke into the Atlanta lineup in 1976 as a catcher/first baseman. In 1983 he led the league in runs batted in, and won back-to-back Most Valuable Player Awards in 1982 and 1983.
Below left: Bob Horner at the plate. James Robert Horner broke in with the Braves in 1978, playing the outfield.
Below right: Dodger pitcher Fernando Valenzuela warms up.

Opposite: Gary Carter at the plate. Gary Edmund Carter came up to the Montreal Expos in 1974 as a catcher/outfielder and hit .407 that year. He then switched to catching. Traded to the Mets for the 1985 season, he immediately became a team leader.

Below: Bruce Sutter, the ace relief pitcher, while he was with the St Louis Cardinals. Breaking in with the Cubs in 1976, he immediately established himself as one of the best firemen of all time. Howard Bruce Sutter won the Cy Young Award with the Cubs in 1979. A rare honor for a relief pitcher.

National League, his 23-11 record gaining him his fourth Cy Young Award (the first pitcher to win that many).

But in the end it was the St Louis Cardinals that took first place, and with no particular stars. The team's total home runs came to only 67 – the lowest for any major league team that year – while one of their pitchers, Jim Kaat, was playing for his 24th straight major league season, a record. But they stole bases – 200 altogether – and got the timely hits, and they beat out Montreal and the Phillies. And then to spoil the Cinderella ending that the Braves were counting on, the Cardinals defeated them in three straight games to take the National League pennant. In the World Series, the Cardinals faced the Milwaukee Brewers, and in a hard-fought slugging duel that went to seven games – with a total of 40 runs for the Cardinals and 33 for the Brewers – the Cardinals came out as World Champions, thanks to some fine pitching by Joaquin Andujar and superb playing by Darrel Porter (named the most valuable player for the Series).

Above: A get-together with former Dodger great Pee Wee Reese (left), Baseball Commissioner Bowie Kuhn (center) and Dodger manager Tommy LaSorda.

Right: Andre Dawson, another speedster for the Montreal Expos. He came up at the end of the 1976 season and made Rookie of the Year in 1978.

The season of 1983 was one of the type that seems to be increasingly more frequent: namely, a year when the action off the diamond threatened to overshadow the game on the field. The whole year, for instance, was marked by the on-going controversy over the dismissal of Bowie Kuhn, as he and some of his supporters made last-ditch efforts to renew his contract; in the end, they failed, but it seemed almost immaterial as he was retained as the interim Commissioner until his successor could be found – and Kuhn went right on exercising to the full all the powers of the Commissioner. In particular, drug and alcohol abuse had now burst onto the scene as a major problem with more and more players, and Kuhn was both praised and attacked for the firm stand – including heavy fines and suspensions – he took against the players whose problems with drugs or alcohol became public.

Another sign of the times was the signing of an agreement in April by which NBC and ABC guaranteed the 26 major league clubs over $1,000,000,000 over six years for telecast rights to games. Since this meant that each team would be guaranteed an average of over $6,000,000 each season even if not one single spectator showed up, it seemed to change the nature of a team's relations with its fans, and taken in conjunction with such developments as Warner Communications' purchase of 48 percent interest in the Pittsburgh Pirates, it seemed to foreshadow a day when baseball games were little more than TV 'productions,' part of some larger entertainment industry. Yet the fact was that by the end of the 1983 season, the 26 major league clubs had once again set a new record for total attendance – 44,587,874 fans had left their TV screens to go out to the ballpark. So perhaps the reports of baseball's demise were a bit premature, after all.

The season itself produced few surprises, although a number of records and all-time stars did figure prominently. In the National League's Eastern Division, the Phillies had first place all for themselves by 28 September, thanks to the performances of such future Hall-of-Famers as Steve Carlton, Joe Morgan and Mike Schmidt. Steve Carlton became only the 16th pitcher in modern baseball to win 300 major league games, while he and Nolan Ryan of the Astros raced neck-and-neck throughout the year to see who would take the all-time lead for strikeouts. Walter Johnson's record of 3508 had been compiled between 1907-27 and it was Nolan Ryan who broke it first, in April; by June, Carlton had overtaken Ryan with his own 3526 strikeouts; the race between these two would go on through 1985.

Another record-breaker was Pete Rose, still with the Phillies and still hot on the trail of several records, including his most coveted, the major-league career hits total; another record race he was forced to abandon was the consecutive games played, when he was benched after playing 745 (leaving him in 10th place for the major leagues). And when the Phillies would offer him a contract only as a part-time player at the end of the season, Rose rejected it, and moved on to start 1984 with the Expos. Meanwhile, Steve Garvey would end his streak of consecutive games played at 1207 on 29 July, when he dislocated his left thumb; it left him in first place in the National League (if considerably behind Lou Gehrig's major league record of 2130).

There was little surprise in the Western Division, either, where the Dodgers took first place. And when the Phillies beat the Dodgers in three out of four games to take the National League pennant, they found themselves facing the Baltimore Orioles in what was a rarity in contemporary baseball – a 'railroad series.' (That is, in an era when teams usually have to jet back and forth to maintain schedules, here were two cities conveniently linked by railroads.) In the end, this didn't help the Phillies, as their stars such as Mike Schmidt fell into a batting slump and the Orioles took the Series, four games to one.

The 1983 season would be remembered for several other highpoints. Bob Forsch of the St Louis Cardinals pitched the second no-hitter of his career. At the end of the season, Johnny Bench retired, as did Gaylord Perry. Jim Kaat, the 44-year-old Cardinals pitcher,

was placed on waivers, which no one picked up; this left Phil Niekro, also at 44, the oldest player in major league baseball, but when he was released by the Braves – after 19 seasons – he was signed up by the Yankees (and was still going strong in 1985).

Finally and most flattering to the National League was a poll taken by *The New York Times* of all active major league players. They voted Steve Carlton of the Phillies as the best pitcher active, Andre Dawson of the Expos as the best all-round ball player and Whitey Herzog as the best manager. So even though the National League lost the All-Star game this year – for the first time in many years – the Nationals could still take pride in their standing in the eyes of all players.

The 1984 season was a 'tale of two cities.' For one, Detroit of the American League, it was 'the best of times.' For the other it was . . . well, if not 'the worst of

Opposite: Steve Carlton, whose Phillies took the pennant in 1983, led the league in strikeouts that year with 275.

Below: Dennis Eckersley pitching for the Chicago Cubs. Dennis Lee Eckersley played for the Indians (1975-77), the Red Sox (1978-83) and then the Cubs. He immediately became a valued member of the starting rotation with the Cubs, with a 10-8 record and a 3.03 earned run average in 1984.

Above: Jodie Davis, the Chicago Cub catcher.
Right: Leon Durham, the Cub first baseman, rounds the bases after hitting a home run. 'Bull' Durham's best year was 1984, when he hit 23 home runs and drove in 96 while batting .279.

Opposite: Ryne Sandberg (top) of the Cubs, although almost taken out of the play by the runner, makes the throw to first to complete a double play. Sandberg hit .314 in 1984, while leading the Cubs, with his hitting and fielding, to the National League East title, becoming the league's Most Valuable Player.

times,' it was certainly a hard year to swallow. That city was the home of a certain National League club that had gone 39 years without getting into any post-season play. Yes, the Cubs of Chicago. And thereby hangs the tale.

As the season was just beginning, *The New York Times* sportswriters picked the Expos to take the Eastern Division and the Dodgers to take the Western Division. So when the Cubs found themselves in an unfamiliar first place in May, they along with the rest of the country were pleasantly surprised. Not that the Cubs didn't have the talent: when the season was over, in fact, Ryne Sandberg of the Cubs was named the most valuable player in the National League, Rick Sutcliffe got the Cy Young award for the league's best pitching and the Cubs' manager, Jim Frey, was voted National League manager of the year.

But there were other teams with plenty of talent, too. The Mets, for instance, had signed Keith Hernandez from the Cardinals and Ray Knight from the Astros; in addition, they had the Rookie of the Year 1983, Daryl Strawberry. Above all, they turned up with an unexpected sensation in Dwight Gooden, who ended up with a 17-9 record but with 251 strikeouts, broke Seaver's old record of 13 games with 10 or more

strikeouts and won Rookie of the Year for his league. One player they did not have was Tom Seaver: at the end of 1982, they had signed him on from Cincinnati, but then, in a monumental blooper, they forgot to add his name to those players to be protected from the free-agent compensation pool – and the Chicago White Sox claimed him in January 1984. Seaver eventually came to terms with the White Sox, as he was determined to keep pitching.

But although the Mets seemed hot at times, they slipped and as the season drew into the final weeks, pennant fever swept Chicago. So confident, in fact, was Chicago that it would win the pennant that an unanticipated controversy arose. The Cubs' home park, Wrigley Field, was the only major league field never to have installed lights for night games, and since the TV networks expect to show at least the midweek Series games at night, there was pressure on the Cubs to install temporary lights at least. But the traditionalists won out: despite all the arguments, the Cubs were not going to play any Series games in Wrigley Field at night.

In fact, the Cubs did not get to play any World Series games in any field nor at any time of day. Oh, they won the Eastern Division by 24 September, their first championship of any kind since 1945. But the San Diego Padres had won the Western Division, and they were no respecters of tradition. The Cubs wiped the Padres out in the first game, 13-0, setting several Series records (including five home runs), and then the Cubs won the second, 4-2. Chicago – indeed, most of the country – could begin to write the headlines proclaiming the Second City Number One. But the next three games were played in San Diego – and the Padres took them, one, two and three.

Opposite far left:
Dwight 'Dr K' Gooden, the phenomenal strikeout artist of the New York Mets.

Above: Thirteen sequence shots showing the smooth delivery of the Great Gooden.
Below: A vendor selling souvenirs in Chicago's Wrigley Field.

So ended the best and worst of years for Chicago. But the whole country had enjoyed the Cubs' race while it lasted. And in the end, the Padres had no chance against the Detroit Tigers, who had led the American League from the first day, wiped out the Oakland A's three straight to take the league pennant, and set down the Padres, four games to one. But the National League had some other memorable occasions for 1984. Pete Rose broke the National league record for career doubles (726) and attained one of his career 'plateaus' – 4097 hits, putting him in second place (behind Ty Cobb's 4191) for all-time major leaguers. And when he left the Expos to return to Cincinnati, where his notable career began, and became a playing-manager, it seemed definite that Rose would go on playing until he took over first place sometime in 1985.

The 1985 season took up pretty much where the 1984 season left off. There was much talk of Pete Rose's virtually certain overtaking of Ty Cobb's long-standing record; indeed, it was predicted that Rose would do so sometime late in August, and when Rose

Opposite: Darryl Strawberry, the young Met outfielder. Strawberry came up to the Mets in 1983 and won the Rookie of the Year Award, primarily for his hitting.
Below: Rick Sutcliffe, the star of the Cub pitching staff, who came to the Cubs early in the 1984 season, and won 16 while losing only one, earning the Cy Young Award.

opened the season with two hits it appeared that he was well on his way. In the end, he tied Cobb on 8 September and then took the lead on 11 September. The other hot topic of the first part of the season was the threatened strike by the players; they did strike on 6 and 7 August, but were back on the field by 8 August (and missed games were made up later).

In other respects the 1985 season had an air of familiarity. The professional sports writers were picking the Cubs and Padres to repeat as winners in

their respective Eastern and Western divisions, but with a major difference: the Cubs were being picked to overcome their jinx and defeat the Padres in the play-offs to go on to the World Series. But in fact, by the midseason All-Star break on 14 July, the Cardinals were in first place in the Eastern Division, with the Mets two and a half games behind (and the Cubs seven and a half games down); while in the Western Division, the Padres trailed the Dodgers by half a game. As the season rolled into September, those four

teams held those same positions – with the gaps only wider.

The 1985 season saw a number of notable records in addition to Pete Rose's. Nolan Ryan, now with the Houston Astros, increased his lead as the all-time strikeout leader by ending the year with 4083. Dwight Gooden, the sensational pitcher for the Mets – already known as 'Doctor K' became the youngest pitcher, at age 20, to gain 20 victories.

And when the 1985 season ended, there were the Cardinals in first place in the Eastern Division and the Dodgers in first place in the Western Division, proving that sports writers could occasionally be wrong. The Cardinals confronted the American League's pennant-winning Kansas City Royals in the World Series, which went to seven games until the Royals emerged as World Champions.

In 1986 the New York Mets finally achieved the success that had eluded them for the previous two

seasons, and with a vengeance. Winning 108 games and clinching the division on 17 September, the Mets displayed both talent and tenacity. Although the Cardinals had taken an early lead, by 23 April the Mets had moved into first place for good; by the mid-season All-Star game, the Mets had a commanding 13-game lead over the Montreal Expos.

In the West a changing of the guard occurred as the Houston Astros, a team picked to finish low in its division, rose to the top. The San Francisco Giants, a team which had finished in the basement in 1985, and the rising star of the Cincinnati Reds, were Houston's challengers, but the Astros would hold them off under Hal Lanier, in his first season as a major league manager.

So the playoffs began with the Astros confronting the Mets. Both were observing their twenty-fifth year (having been expansion teams of 1962) but the resemblence seemed to end there – the Mets, on paper at least, looking far the stronger. Not only did they boast those 108 wins, they had outscored their opponents by 181 runs, while the Astros had outscored theirs by only 71. Houston did have some solid pitching, not only from all-time great, Nolan Ryan, but from the underrated Mike Scott, plus Bob Knepper, Jim Deshaies and relievers Dave Smith and Charlie Kerfeld. For hitting, the Astros could count on Kevin Bass, Davey Lopes, Glen Davis and Jose Cruz. But the Mets could more than match these, with strong pitching from Dwight Gooden, Ron Darling, Sid Fernandez and Bob Ojeda, and with Roger McDowell and Jesse Orosco standing by for relief. And for hitting, the Mets could count on Keith Hernandez, Darryl Strawberry, Gary Carter, Lenny Dykstra and Ray Knight. The consensus was that, as good as the Astros were, the Mets were better.

But the playoffs were no pushover. The Astros took the first game, in fact, 1-0, thanks to Mike Scott's masterful pitching, but the Mets quickly came back to take the second, 5-1. The Series moved to Shea Stadium, where the Mets won again, thanks to Lenny Dykstra's ninth-inning homer. But in the fourth game, Mike Scott led the Astros to another win, 3-1. In the fifth and sixth games, the Mets were able to summon up all their superior reserves, but they had to work for their wins – 12 innings in the fifth, while the sixth was an exciting 16-inning epic that the Mets won 7-6, to take the pennant.

The Mets went into the World Series against the Red Sox as the favorite (except throughout New England) and everyone was unsettled when the Boston team took the first two games in Shea Stadium. Up in Fenway Park, however, the Mets also ran counter to the odds and took the next two. The teams went back to Shea with the Red Sox having won three of the five games. And when in the sixth game the Red Sox came into the ninth inning with a 2-0 lead, it looked like the Mighty Mets were about to concede the championship to the Amazin' Red Sox. But a combination of poor pitching and bad fielding on the part of Boston, plus scratch hitting and baserunning by the Mets, allowed the Mets to tie the game in the bottom of the ninth inning. The Red Sox got two more runs in the top of the tenth, but the Mets came back in the bottom to score three themselves and take the game. Play resumed after a day's postponement due to rain, which allowed Boston to start Bruce Hurst, who had already beaten the Mets in two games. The Mets soon found themselves behind, 3-0, but they caught up, then went ahead on Ray Knight's homer, and added four more runs to win the game 8-5, and the Series. So the Mets came through, and their championship was all the sweeter for having had to come from behind.

Individual National Leaguers could also look back on the 1986 season with considerable satisfaction. Bob Horner of the Atlanta Braves, for one, became only the eleventh player in modern major-league baseball to hit four homers in one game (on 6 July). Steve Carlton, although he was dropped by the Phillies early in the season, signed on with the San Francisco Giants but then retired near the end of the season – his 4,040 strikeouts putting him in second place for career strikeouts (behind Nolan Ryan's 4,277 through 1986), while 323 victories put him squarely in tenth place among all of modern baseball's pitchers. One of the biggest news items of the season was the appointment of the recently retired president of Yale University, A Bartlett Giamatti, as new president of the National League – a sign, it might be said, of the

special role that baseball has come to play in American society.

The National League began its 1987 season under not one cloud but three. To begin with, there was the charge of collusion on the part of all major-league club owners. For at least the last three years, it was alleged, they had in one way or another been conspiring to stop bidding for free agents in an effort to force players to settle for smaller salaries. The charge was placed in arbitration. On 21 September 1987 it was ruled that the owners had been engaged in some sort of collusion. But aside from the question of what would now be done to right this wrong, it was hard to prove if this had had any identifiable impact on team standings. Some of the free agents simply returned to their former teams – Tim Raines, for instance – but others were so angry that their owners hadn't bid for them that they jumped to other teams for considerably lower salaries (Ray Knight to the Orioles, for instance, and Andre Dawson to the Cubs). Bob Horner of the Braves was so angry that he went all the way to Japan, where he became something of a cult figure.

Then there was the charge of racism that came about primarily through the actions of a National League executive. Al Campanis of the Los Angeles Dodgers' front office went on national TV in April as part of the observation of the 40th anniversary of Jackie Robinson's having joined the Dodgers – but Campanis ended up making some incredible remarks about blacks lacking the proper capacity to hold management or administrative positions. Before the

Above: The 1986 National League Cy Young Award winner Mike Scott.

dust settled Campanis was fired by the Dodgers, but ironically he had succeeded in calling attention to a glaring flaw in the structure of organized baseball: Blacks (and Hispanics) were not being allowed to hold any significant posts except as players. The resolution of this deep-seated problem lies many years in the future but at least it is now out in the open.

The third problem was one that had been around for a while and also was not going to go away soon: drugs. It was thrown into the spotlight at the very start of the season by the discovery that Dwight Gooden, the Mets' young superstar pitcher, had come up positive in a test for cocaine. Gooden went into a drug clinic immediately, but the message was clear: A lot of ballplayers were probably still using drugs and the problem – like those of money and racism – was not going to be solved in one season.

Even with the loss of Gooden for the first weeks, the Mets were generally conceded to have a chance of taking at least the pennant after their 1986 championship. But the Mets' pitchers and hitters never quite put it all together. Hitting home runs was not the problem: The Mets' Howard Johnson was hitting so many that he was one of several players accused of using 'corked' (that is, doctored) bats, but in fact it was never proven. In any case, the Mets never even dominated their own division. The St Louis Cardinals, instead, took over first place and gradually made it clear they were going all the way. The Cardinals lacked the power hitters and the super pitchers of other teams, but they played a scrappy base-running game, and by the time the Mets came up against the Cardinals on the last weekend of the season the Cardinals had clinched the division title. The Montreal Expos, meanwhile, surprised many by also staying up there with the Mets until the end.

In the Western Division the Cincinnati Reds were singled out by many as the team to watch. Sure

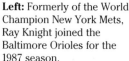

Left: Formerly of the World Champion New York Mets, Ray Knight joined the Baltimore Orioles for the 1987 season.

Below left: Howard Johnson of the New York Mets hit so many home runs in 1987 that he was accused of using a 'corked' bat. The allegation was never proven.

Above: Tim Raines became a free agent in 1987, but wound up rejoining his old team, the Montreal Expos.

enough, the Reds raced out of the starting gate with an 18-8 record. Pete Rose, their manager, chose not to activate himself at the outset, stating that he'd wait to see what the team's needs were later in the season. In the end, he never did activate himself, so for now Rose remains unofficially retired (and his 4256 hits remain the all-time record). Perhaps Rose should have taken a more active role, because something happened to the Reds: on 7 August they were leading the San Francisco Giants by five games; over the next 19 days the Reds went 5-15, while the Giants went 15-5, and on 26 August their situations were reversed. The Reds never could recover, and the Giants ended up with the Western Division title.

Going into the playoffs the Giants were considered the underdogs. True, they had several strong players – Will Clark, Candy Maldonado, Jeffrey Leonard, Kevin Mitchell, Jose Uribe, along with solid pitchers like Mike Krukow, Rick Reuschel and Dave Dravecky. But many felt they were no match for the more experienced Cardinals – Ozzie Smith, Willie McGee, Vince Coleman, Tony Pena and pitchers such as John Tudor, Danny Cox and Todd Worrell. But the Giants went out in front and had a 3-2 game advantage. It took all the talents the Cardinals could muster to even the series in the sixth game with a 1-0 score and then go on to take the seventh game and the pennant.

In the World Series the Cardinals faced the Minnesota Twins, and although the Cardinals were certainly the more experienced team, they were going to be without the injured Jack Clark, one of their heaviest hitters, while another, Terry Pendleton, would not be able to play at full strength. When the Twins took the first two games it looked like the Cardinals' brand of scrappy hitting and running might not be a match for the big bats of the Twins. Then the Cardinals came back and took the next three games in St Louis. But the Twins were able to do what no other team had ever done in the 31 years that the Series had gone to seven games – win all their home games. Even though many observers felt the Metrodome gave the Twins a special advantage (with its distracting lighting, high-decibel acoustics and general artificiality), all agreed that the Cardinals had fought to the finish, even if they were beaten for the World Championship.

As for individual records during the National League's 1987 season, who should end up with the most home runs – 49 – but Andre Dawson, the same Dawson who had left the Expos in disgust to play with the Cubs for a reduced salary. Dawson also had the most RBIs (137) for the majors. Tony Gwynne of the Padres had the best batting average, .369, for both leagues, and Vince Coleman's 107 stolen bases far and away led both leagues. As it happened, no National League pitcher won 20 games, but veteran Nolan Ryan ended up with the best earned run average (2.76) and most strikeouts (270). The league's MVP was Andre Dawson, while Steve Bedrosian won the Cy Young award. One of the more remarkable performances of the season was that of San Diego's rookie catcher, Benito Santiago, who hit safely in 34 games.

And so the National League continued as it had since its year of organization, 1876, providing thrills and surprises – yes, and occasional disappointments. True, there were some major problems threatening major league baseball: the cases of drug and alcohol abuse; the skyrocketing salaries that were leading some club owners to claim they were on the verge of bankruptcy; increasingly more open conflicts between players and owners. But major league baseball had a new commissioner, Peter Ueberroth, who had

Above: Speedy Ozzie Smith was one of the stars of the 1987 St Louis Cardinals, winners of the National League pennant.
Right: Pete Rose, manager of the Cincinnati Reds, chose not to activate himself in 1987 and was sorely missed by his team. After a strong start, the Reds ended up seeing the San Francisco Giants take the Western Division title.

Opposite: Mets' ace pitcher Dwight Gooden tested positive for cocaine early in the 1987 season and had to go into a drug rehabilitation clinic for a month.

Above: Nolan Ryan of the Houston Astros had the best ERA (2.76) and most strikeouts (270) of any pitcher in the National League in 1987.
Right: World Series action: the St Louis Cardinals versus the Minnesota Twins. The Twins took the Series, four games to three.
Bottom: Another stolen base for Vince Coleman of the St Louis Cardinals. His 1987 total of 107 stolen bases was the best by far in both leagues.

taken over on 1 October 1984, after his dazzling success as president of the Los Angeles Olympic Organizing Committee, and Ueberroth gave every indication of providing strong yet fair leadership.

Before the 1988 National League season began most experts predicted that the New York Mets would walk away with the National League pennant and face the Yankees in a Subway Series. A month later the Pirates and the Dodgers led their respective divisions, but by the All-Star break the Mets had indeed captured first place in the East and looked like they intended to keep it. Sparked by a great season from hurler Orel Hershiser, in the National League West the Dodgers finished on top of a division they had dominated from the get-go.

Considerable controversy was generated prior to the season when major league baseball announced its intention to strictly enforce the balk rule. Balk calls due to closer scrutiny of the pitchers' 'set' position

rose 160 percent during the season, quickly wiping out the combined-league season record of 356. But the dire effects on the outcomes of games due to strict enforcement of the balk rule that some had predicted never materialized, and the issue gradually faded from the sports pages.

Meanwhile home runs dropped 29 percent from 1987's record-setting pace. Team batting averages and ERAs also declined, leading some to wonder if the ball had been made less lively. Despite some convincing statistical evidence to the contrary, the consensus was that improved pitching accounted for the drops. Other rule changes empowered umpires to choose between warning and expulsion when a pitcher threw intentionally at a batter; and catchers were required to wear helmets when fielding their positions.

Behind stingy pitching and booming bats – Darryl Strawberry led the league with 39 home runs – the Mets clinched the Eastern Division title, only to be stopped by the Dodgers in a seven-game championship series. The Dodgers' Orel Hershiser, who had smoked through the regular season with 23 wins, 8 shutouts and a record 59 scoreless innings, took two games from the Mets, including a five-hit shutout, with some able assistance from slugging MVP teammate Kirk Gibson. In addition to receiving the Cy Young Award, Hershiser was voted both league champion-

Right: Dodger ace Orel Hershiser had a banner year in 1988. The Cy Young Award winner also garnered NLCS and World Series MVP honors.

ship MVP and World Series MVP for his part in a classic Dodger performance that saw Tommy Lasorda's bums drop the highly favored Oakland Athletics in five games.

In July arbitrator George Nicolau found the owners guilty in the second collusion case the players brought against them for their conspiracy not to sign free agents (in 1986-87). A. Bartlett Giamatti, who had resigned the presidency of Yale to become president of the National League at the end of the 1986 season, was chosen to succeed Peter Ueberroth as commissioner of baseball. And in 1988 Chicago's Wrigley Field, the last holdout in the majors, finally installed lights and hosted its first night game.

The 1989 season saw some major upheavals in the National League. At the beginning of spring training, former Cincinnati superstar, player-manager, and current manager Pete Rose was summoned to the commissioner's office to answer allegations of gambling. Despite Rose's repeated denials and challenges to Commissioner Giamatti's right to judge his case, the special counsel appointed by Giamatti concluded that Rose had indeed bet on baseball and on the Reds, and Giamatti suspended Rose from involvement with organized baseball for life.

Eight days later, on 1 September, Giamatti, age 51, who had served less than five months as commissioner, died of a heart attack. He was succeeded by his hand-picked Deputy Commissioner Fay Vincent. Bill White, a former Golden Glove National League player and Yankee broadcaster, became the first black league president and the highest ranking black sports

official in American history when he filled the National League presidency that Giamatti had vacated when he ascended to the commissionership on 1 April. In May, superstar Mike Schmidt hung up his glove with a tearful good-bye.

The pundits picked the Mets to top the National League East, but to the pleased surprise of many, the Chicago Cubs soon took over first place and hung onto it. Out West, San Francisco fended off threats from the Padres and the Astros to take the Western

Above left: Baseball Commissioner A. Bartlett Giamatti died suddenly and unexpectedly in September 1989, after serving less than five months in office.
Above: Fay Vincent succeeded Giamatti as baseball commissioner in 1989.

Division. Despite a strong pitching staff, the Cubs were unable to silence the bats of Giants Kevin Mitchell, Will Clark and Matt Williams, and the Giants took the pennant from the Cubs in five games. League MVP Mitchell logged 47 home runs, 125 RBIs, and a .635 slugging average; playoff MVP Clark batted a blistering .333 with 196 hits, 104 runs, and 111 RBIs.

San Francisco met Oakland in a 'BART' (Bay Area Rapid Transit) Subway Series dedicated to – and nicknamed after – the recently deceased 'Bart' Giamatti. In the first two games the Giants fell to the pitching of Dave Stewart and Mike Moore. Then on 17 October, at Candlestick Park, just 26 minutes before the start of the third game, the Bay Area was hit by a major earthquake that killed 63. Observed Giant centerfielder Brett Butler, 'At the start I realized what a privilege it was to be in the Series. Now, I realize what a privilege it is to be alive.' Ten days later the Series resumed. Oakland's pitchers of the first two games repeated

their magic, and the Giants fell in four.

After a 32-day lockout by the owners during spring training, the 1990 National League season got underway with Lou Piniella at the helm of a Cincinnati team still smarting from the loss of Pete Rose. Once again the Mets were heavily favored for divisional and pennant honors, but the Pittsburgh Pirates, behind the slugging of Barry Bonds and Bobby Bonilla, who combined for 65 home runs and 235 RBIs, and the pitching of a no-name bullpen headed by Doug Drabek and Zane Smith, sewed up the division in a three-game sweep of the Mets in September. Drabek, with 22 regular season wins, took the Cy Young Award. MVP Bonds batted .301, slugged .565 with 33 homers and 114 RBIs, and scored 104 runs. At 40 round-trippers, Cub Ryne Sandberg became the first second baseman to lead the league in homers since Rogers Hornsby.

Lou Piniella's reinvigorated Reds, with his Nasty Boys leading the bullpen, topped the Western Division

Opposite top: The lights are switched on for the first night game at Chicago's Wrigley Field on 8 August 1988.

Left: The Giants' heavy-hitting Will Clark springs out of the batter's box. Clark's NLCS MVP performance in 1989 helped San Francisco take the pennant from the Cubs.

Right: The scene at Candlestick Park moments after an earthquake interrupted the start of the 1989 World Series' game there. The Bayside World Series between the Oakland Athletics and the San Francisco Giants was resumed after an 11-day hiatus.

Below: Pittsburgh's Doug Drabek, winner of the 1990 Cy Young Award, also helped his Pirates win their division in 1991.

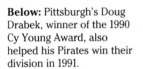

five games ahead of the Dodgers, then fulfilled the promise they had been unable to realize during the preceding years by stopping the Bucs in the playoff in six games. In a decisive Series upset, Cincinnati swept the defending Athletics. The Reds' Billy Hatcher set an all-time Series batting average record of .750, while Cincinnati's batters averaged .317 overall and slugged .472 for the four games. Series MVP Jose Rijo won two of the games by following the Reds' strategy of pitching fastballs inside, which seemed to unnerve Oakland's sluggers.

As the National League entered the last decade of the 20th century, the age-old struggle between players and owners closed another chapter when the players' third collusion grievance against the owners for conspiring against free-agency was decided in their favor. The owners agreed to pay the Players Association a total settlement of $280 million. The contract negotiations that precipitated the spring lockout ended with a new Basic Agreement that raised a player's minimum salary from $68,000 to $100,000, and prescribed triple damages for any future owner collusion concerning free agents. Pete Rose was sentenced to five months in federal prison and fined $50,000 for tax evasion.

The 1991 season got underway with a pre-season umpire strike that ended hours before the first game. The real news, however, was in the National League West, acknowledged the toughest division in the majors, where the upstart Atlanta Braves snatched the division championship from the Dodgers on the second-to-last day of the season. While their fans waved thousands of foam-rubber tomahawks in the 'tomahawk chop' and sang an eerie 'war chant,' the Miracle Braves, who lagged nine and a half games behind the Dodgers at the All-Star break, put together an eight-game end-of-season winning streak that was all the more remarkable because they had finished last in the previous three seasons. Atlanta's dramatic turnaround was sparked by sluggers Ron Gant and

MVP Terry Pendleton, who totaled 54 home runs between them; by 20-game winner Tom Glavine; and by young pitching phenomenon Steve Avery and hurlers Charlie Leibrandt and John Smoltz. David Cone of the Mets, in the last regular game of the year, matched the league record of 19 strikeouts and tied the season's major league strikeout record of 241 in his tenth career shutout.

Once again the drug issue came to the fore when the Braves' star outfielder, Otis Nixon, batting .297 and leading the league with 72 steals, tested positive for cocaine and was suspended for 60 days late in the season. But his absence didn't stop the Braves from snatching the pennant from the Pittsburgh Pirates in a seven-game playoff that featured two brilliant shutouts by series MVP Avery, one by teammate Smoltz, and a new NLCS record of seven steals by Ron Gant. Pittsburgh's second pennant disappointment in as many years paved the way for the Braves to meet the

Minnesota Twins in the World Series – Atlanta's first ever Series appearance. The Twins and the Braves shared honors as the first teams to go from last place to first place in the 22 years of division play.

In one of the most thrilling World Series in memory, the Braves battled the favored Twins through seven games. Five games were decided by one run, four in the last at-bat, four in the last inning, and three reached extra innings. Atlanta won all three home games, Minnesota all four of theirs. In the seventh game, the Twins scored the game's only run in the bottom of the tenth. It was baseball at its best, a Series that not only went the limit, but went into legend. Atlanta's Lonnie Smith hit home runs in three consecutive games, and teammate Mark Lemke turned in the kind of surprising virtuoso performance that postseason play is known for. Off the field, the old Negro Leagues were honored in a special ceremony in Cooperstown, and National League president Bill

White spoke out forcefully when the new Colorado Rockies franchise filled six upper-level executive positions without even interviewing a black or Latino candidate despite promises to do so.

The announcement during the 1991 season that the National League's two new franchises – to commence playing in 1993 – would be assigned to Denver, Colorado, and Miami, Florida, caused only a mild flurry of excitement at first. But before the 1992 season ended the new teams would play a pivotal role in a major crisis within organized baseball. But none of this had any impact on the National League as the 1992 season got underway. Of more interest to the fans were several major 'jumps' by star players – Eddie Murray went from the Dodgers to the Mets, Eric Davis went to the Dodgers from the Reds, Bret Saberhagen went from the Kansas City Royals to the Mets, and Bobby Bonilla went from the Pirates to the Mets.

Indeed, with all those powerhouse (and expensive:

Above left: In 1991 the Braves' Ron Gant set a new NLCS record for steals, with seven, as Atlanta downed Pittsburgh in seven games.
Above: Atlanta's David Justice connects for a home run against the Twins' Scot Erickson in game three of the 1991 World Series.

Right: Bobby Bonilla
displays his new uniform
after signing a six-year
contract for $28 million
with the New York Mets.
Bonilla is flanked by the
Mets' general manager Al
Harazin (l) and manager
Jeff Torborg (r). Bonilla's
three-year-old daughter,
Danielle, crouches below.

Below: The Atlanta Braves'
catcher Damon Berryhill
tags out the Blue Jays' Pat
Borders at the plate during
the fourth inning of game
six of the 1992 World
Series. Borders was named
the Series' Most Valuable
Player.

Bonilla was given a six-year contract for $28 million,
making him temporarily the highest paid player in the
history of baseball) additions, the Mets looked like a
distinct threat to take over at least the Eastern Division. But the Mets never really got going, for whatever
mixture of excuses, and it was the Pirates who took
the division for the third straight year, having held on
to first place for all but 10 days of the season. Their
main – and only – threat right up until 27 September,
in fact, were not the Mets but the Montreal Expos.

In the Western Division, there was a bit more of a
contest. At the outset, the Braves were picked by
many to repeat – assuming that the stellar 1991 performances of Terry Pendleton, Tom Glavine, and

Steve Avery weren't falling stars – but the Cincinnati
Reds were seen by many others as the more powerful
team. By the All-Star break, the Reds were indeed in
first place, but the Braves soon began to move ahead.
They pushed the Padres back in line, took over first,
and remained there to the end – although they did not
actually clinch it until 29 September.

For the third straight year the Pirates found themselves in the playoffs for the league pennant and for
the second straight year they were facing the Braves.
And Atlanta was determined to prove that their 1991
victory wasn't some statistical fluke. The Pirates were
probably favored on the grounds of experience and
sheer statistical probability: how many years in a row
can one team blow the league championship? The
world was soon to see. The Braves – playing true team
ball, with no fancy stars or heroics – quickly took
command and suddenly the Pirates were down, three
games to one. In the fifth game, Barry Bonds came
alive and the Pirates won. In the sixth game, the
Pirates racked up eight runs in the second inning and
went on to win 13-4. Now it was the classic situation: a
whole season come down to one game. Behind ace
Doug Drabek, the Pirates moved out to a 2-0 lead that
held up until the bottom of the ninth. Many Atlanta
patrons had actually left the stadium when Pendleton
led off with a double. Soon the bases were loaded,
Drabek was gone and Stan Belinda was in at relief.
Pendleton got home on a sacrifice fly and then
Francisco Cabrera – whose entire major league 1992
season involved only 10 at-bats – hit a single to left
bringing home David Justice and Sid Bream with the
tying and winning runs. The Braves – and the Pirates –
had done it again!

In the World Series for the second straight year, the
Braves found themselves meeting the Toronto Blue
Jays. Depending on whom you listened to, either team
was favored. Though the Braves took the first game
with Tom Glavine going all the way, they then lost the
next two when Jeff Reardon gave up a two-run homer

to Ed Sprague in the ninth inning in game two and a tie-breaking run to Candy Maldonado in the ninth of game three. When the Blue Jays won game four and led the Series three games to one the Braves were all but written off. But they came back in game five and with the aid of Lonnie Smith's grand slam home run in the fifth inning, won 7-2. So it was back to Atlanta for game six; by two-outs in the bottom of the ninth, the Blue Jays were just hanging on to a 2-1 lead, when Otis Nixon managed to get a hit that sent Jeff Blauser home with the tying run. The Braves fans were now chopping and chanting like true believers, but Dave Winfield put Toronto ahead with a two-run double in the top of the 11th. The Braves got one run back but Otis Nixon's surprise bunt with two out failed and the Braves lost, 4-3. In fact, the Braves had lost all four games by only one run, so all agreed that they had nothing to be ashamed of.

For several National League members, 1992 would be a season to remember. Barry Bonds got the MVP and Greg Maddux was Cy Young winner. Barry Bonds had his second 30-30 season (34 homers, 39 stolen bases), but what made it especially sweet is that among the few he joined in that elite circle (only four others!) of those who have done this more than once is Bobby Bonds, his own father. Nolan Ryan continued to put his career strikeout total ever farther beyond the reach of mortals, ending up with 5,668. And Mickey Morandi, second baseman with the Philadelphia Phillies took a place in the record book with his unassisted triple play against the Pirates on 20 September – only the fourth in National League history (and just the ninth in all of organized baseball history).

As for the commotion arising from the new franchises, they turned out to be one of the contributing factors leading to the resignation of Fay Vincent, the commissioner of baseball only since September 1989, when A. Bartlett Giamatti died unexpectedly. Vincent had not seemed the kind who was going to provoke

confrontations, but his handling of several issues began to rankle certain club owners. The last straw came when he unilaterally announced that, with the two new teams joining the league, he would restructure the divisions. In particular, he intended to place the Chicago Cubs in the Western Division, which not only angered the Cubs' owner and Cub fans, but upset enough of the other major league club owners so that a majority gave Vincent what was effectively a vote of no confidence. Although he maintained that legally they had no right to depose him, Vincent knew that he

could no longer function effectively, and in September he stepped down. Until a new commissioner was named, 'Bud' Selig, owner of the Milwaukee Brewers, was named as interim chairperson of organized baseball.

Before the 1993 season began on the field, the owners of the major league clubs made news as they continued to refuse to name a commissioner to replace Fay Vincent and, in February, voted to ban Marge Schott, owner of the Cincinnati Reds, from the day-to-day operations of her team for a year and fined her $25,000 for using 'ethnic slurs.' Still, there was a certain amount of excitement among all National League fans as the 1993 season commenced with the addition of two new clubs, the Colorado Rockies and the Florida Marlins – the first teams to be added to the league since the Montreal Expos and San Diego Padres joined in 1969.

In the National League East, there was not much suspense throughout the season as the Phillies, who had finished last in their division the previous year, moved into first place at the outset of the season and remained there. Meanwhile, the Mets turned in a dismal performance with the worst winning percentage in the majors for 1993 (.364), falling into last place in their division behind even the rookie Florida Marlins.

In the National League West there was some surprise when the San Francisco Giants quickly took over first place; by the All Star break they had a 9-game lead

Left: The National League's 1992 Cy Young Award-winner, Greg Maddux of the Chicago Cubs. Maddux went on to win the award in 1993 and 1994 as well, with the Atlanta Braves.
Above: The Pittsburgh Pirates' Barry Bonds won his second MVP Award in 1992. Bonds was ranked first in seven statistical categories including runs (109), walks (127), on-base percentage (.456), slugging percentage (.624), and extra-base hits (75).

Above: Lee Smith began with the Chicago Cubs in 1980, became a reliever in 1982, led the league with saves in 1983 and then quietly but steadily saved game after game. After two full years with the Red Sox (1988-89) he moved over to St Louis in May 1990 and in the 1993 season took over the all-time saves record from Jeff Reardon.

Above right: The son of Bobby Bonds, Barry has had a lot to live up to and has more than done so since starting with the Pirates in 1986. Playing left field, he proved to be a superb fielder as well as an exciting hitter, winning four Golden Glove awards and three MVPs by 1993. That year he signed a record-breaking $46 million five-year contract with the Giants.

and at one point in August they moved to a 10-game lead over the second-place Braves. But by mid-September the Atlanta Braves had taken over first place and the Giants were four games out. In the final days of the season, the Giants closed the gap, game by game, and with the next-to-last game the Braves and Giants were tied for first, each with a remarkable 103 wins, a record for both leagues in the 1993 season. On the final day the Giants found themselves playing their arch rivals, the Dodgers, who were only too happy to be the spoilers. Meanwhile, the Braves met the inexperienced Colorado Rockies and had an easy day on the field. For the third year in a row, the Braves were back in the playoffs.

In the league championship series, the Braves were favored by all the non-sentimentalists, given their recent experience in post-season play and their team stats. The Phillies were definitely the underdogs in every sense: unpolished, unshaven, unruly, and untested. Indeed, the mighty Braves did out-hit and out-score the Phillies during the six games they played, but the Phillies got the extra runs when they needed them and took the National League championship, 4-2. So the Phillies had done just what the Braves had done in 1991 – come from last place in their division the year before to take the pennant.

In the World Series, the Phillies were once again the upstarts, facing the reigning world champions, the Toronto Blue Jays. Toronto took the first game, 8-5, but the Phillies bounced back and took the second, 6-4, thanks to Jim Eisenreich's three-run homer. Moving to Philadelphia, the Blue Jays took the third, 10-3, with a stellar performance from veteran Paul Molitor.

But it was the fourth game that would go down in the history books as one of the wildest games ever

played. The marathon match lasted 4 hours, 14 minutes – the longest in post-season play. The Blues got three runs in the top of the first, but the Phillies came right back with four, and from then on the hits and runs kept coming, ending with a combined 31 hits (with no official errors) and a final score of 15-14, Toronto's favor: the highest-scoring post-season game in major league history.

Many expected the Phillies to have been so devastated by that loss that they would just fold, but instead it was the Toronto Blue Jays who seemed shell-shocked by their performance the night before, and the Phillies won game five, 2-0, behind Curt Schilling's five-hit shutout. It was back to Toronto for game six, and right through to the bottom of the ninth inning, Phillies' supporters had reason to believe in a storybook comeback. But then Mitch 'Wild Thing' Williams came in as relief, and before he knew it two men were on – and then Joe Carter hit a line drive over the left field fence. This was only the second time in baseball history that a World Series had been decided by a home run. Toronto took the game, 8-6, and the World Series, the first team to win back-to-back titles since the 1977-1978 Yankees.

But if the Phillies lost the Series, they held the respect of all lovers of baseball – and none deserved it more than Lenny Dykstra, coming off a year that put him in close contention for MVP. Other National League players who would look back on 1993 with special pride were Darryl Kite of the Astros, who pitched a no-hitter, and Mark Whiten of the Cardinals, who hit four homers and drove in 12 runs in one game, tying two major league marks and coming up with one of the most productive days in the history of the game.

Another amazing record: the Colorado Rockies

shattered all previous season figures with 4,483,350 tickets sold. Both expansion teams, by the way, avoided finishing in last place in their divisions – the Rockies beating out the decimated Padres, and the Marlins coming in ahead of the hapless Mets. As for the 'thin' air of Denver, which many thought might greatly affect games played there, it did not seem to make that much of a difference. The fact is that the 1993 season saw quite a large jump in home runs throughout both leagues – a whopping 55 percent increase over 1992's totals in the National League and a 16.8 percent increase in the American League.

When the 1994 season began, there were hints of a possible strike, but that hardly seemed the issue to most fans. The real issue seemed to be the problems raised by dividing the leagues into three divisions. Who could keep track of them? What would standings mean when a second-place team would become the fourth team in the playoffs? And how would fans feel if such a team went on to win the World Series? As it turned out, fans needn't have worried.

It did help, though, to have a program to keep track of the new lineups. The National League East now includes the Atlanta Braves, Philadelphia Phillies, Montreal Expos, Florida Marlins and New York Mets. The National League West is now made up of the San

Left: Righthander Curt Schilling began with the Orioles in 1988, and after spending 1991 with the Astros, came into his own when he joined the Phillies in 1992. In 1993 he had a 16-7 season that helped his team to take the league championship, and pitched a memorable five-hit shutout in the fifth game of the World Series.
Below: John Kruk began with San Diego in 1986, then moved to the Phillies during the 1989 season. Kruk caught the fans' fancy with his rough-hewn appearance and roughhouse style. He posted his personal best in 1992 – a .323 BA – while the Phillies finished last in their division, but in 1993 he was one of the crew that led the Phillies into the World Series.

Above: Coming up to the Giants in 1987, Matt Wiliams took over at third base while gradually improving his batting average and home run production, hitting 38 in 1993. In 1994 he seemed to be on course to take over the season home run record, but when the season abruptly ended on 11 August, he had to settle for a major league leading 43.

Above right: Standout first baseman Fred McGriff began with the Blue Jays (1986-90) and after starting 1991 with San Diego, joined the Atlanta Braves during the 1993 season. A power-hitter, he led the AL in 1989 with 36 homers, then led the NL in 1992 with 35.

Francisco Giants, Los Angeles Dodgers, Colorado Rockies, and San Diego Padres. The new Central Division includes the St Louis Cardinals, Houston Astros, Chicago Cubs, Pittsburgh Pirates, and Cincinnati Reds.

In the National League East, the Braves were once again picked by many to repeat as first in the division for a fourth consecutive year, with either the Phillies or the Expos expected to give them a race. By the All Star break, the Expos had moved one game ahead of the Braves. In the National League West, 1994 was generally viewed as a race between San Francisco and Los Angeles, with most sports reporters giving the edge to the Giants. If anyone ever needed reminding of the fallibility of sports predictions, it was this race, for as the Giants struggled, then faded, the Dodgers did indeed move ahead, but it was the upstart Rockies that moved into second place. In the new Central Division, opinion was divided between the Reds and the Astros. At the All Star break, the Reds held a 2-½ game lead over the Padres.

As the season moved into its second half, the Expos (with the second lowest payroll in the majors) took a solid 6-game lead over the Braves, the Giants displaced the Rockies behind the Dodgers, and the Astros were only a half-game behind the Reds. But the players went out on strike on 12 August, and neither they nor the owners would concede anything over the major issue of a salary cap. The owners argued that there were too many teams that were losing money because they did not have enough local TV and other revenue. The owners' solution was to put a 'cap' on the total amount paid in salaries by each team – the practice in pro basketball and football. The players

saw this as a thinly disguised way to limit their salaries – and just as important, as a way for the owners to avoid resolving their own problems. Indeed, the owners had a lot to answer for by not having chosen a new independent Commissioner: the acting Commissioner, Bud Selig, was himself an owner of a team (the Brewers) and was certainly not the man to order players and owners to get back on the field 'for the good of the game.'

Despite a last-minute effort in early September to revive negotiations, the 1994 season came to a dismaying end. Talk of a 'juiced' ball contributing to the high number of home runs had long faded, and the three-division race format had, at least superficially, added some excitement by providing three separate races. Individuals like Matt Williams of the Giants, who was vying for the all-time home run record, and 1994 MVP Jeff Bagwell of the Astros, who was in contention for the Triple Crown, were especially hurt by the season's abrupt end. Barry Bonds was having another great year, as were pitchers Greg Maddux of the Braves (the 1993 and 1994 Cy Young Award winner) and Ken Hill of the Expos. Although the minor leagues satisfied some of the fans' attention, no one pretended it was the same as the major league pennant race.

Not since the White Sox scandal of 1919 had major league baseball left such a bitter taste in the mouths of fans. And for the first time since 1904, there was no World Series. Few were predicting what would happen in 1995, but everyone knew that baseball was going to have to find some way of bouncing back. It always has. The National League, baseball's senior league, was not about to let the National Pastime vanish.

INDEX

Photo Credits

All photographs courtesy The National Baseball Library, Cooperstown, New York, except the following:
Marcello Bertinetti: 116.
Nancy Hogue: 93, 99, 102, 103, 105, 109, 110-111(bottom), 111(top right), 112(both), 113, 115, 117, 119, 120, 121, 124, 126, 127(right), 130(bottom), 131(both), 132.
Library of Congress: 27.
Ron Modra: 1, 122, 123, 125(both), 127(left), 128, 129, 133, 134(both), 135, 136(left), 136-137(top, center), 138, 139, 140-141(both), 142, 143, 144, 145(all three), 146, 147(both), 148(all three).
Ponzini Photography: 2-3, 149, 150(bottom right), 151, 152(bottom), 153(left), 155(both), 156(both), 157(bottom), 158(both).
Bruce L. Schwartzman: 150(bottom center).
UPI/Bettmann Newsphotos: 150(top), 152(top), 153(right), 154(both), 157(top).
Angela White: 137(bottom).